Series / Number 07-030

TEST ITEM BIAS

STEVEN J. OSTERLIND
Oakland Unified School District

SAGE PUBLICATIONS
The International Professional Publishers
Newbury Park   London   New Delhi

For information address:

SAGE Publications, Inc.
2455 Teller Road
Newbury Park, California 91320
E-mail: order@sagepub.com

SAGE Publications Ltd.
6 Bonhill Street
London EC2A 4PU
United Kingdom

SAGE Publications India Pvt. Ltd.
M-32 Market
Greater Kailash I
New Delhi 110 048 India

International Standard Book Number 0-8039-1989-1

Library of Congress Catalog Card No. L.C. 83-060129

99   00   01   02   03   15   14   13   12   11   10

When citing a professional paper, please use the proper form. Remember to cite the correct
Sage University Paper series title and include the paper number. One of the two following
formats can be adapted (depending on the style manual used):

(1) IVERSEN, GUDMUND R. and NORPOTH, HELMUT (1976) "Analysis of Variance." Sage University Paper series on Quantitative Applications in the Social Sciences,
07-001. Beverly Hills: Sage Publications.

OR

(2) Iversen, Gudmund R. and Norpoth, Helmut. 1976. *Analysis of Variance.* Sage
University Paper series on Quantitative Applications in the Social Sciences, series no.
07-001. Beverly Hills: Sage Publications.

CONTENTS

107058

Series Editor's Introduction

Dr. Osterlind defines an *unbiased* test item as one for which the probability of success is the same for equally able test takers of the same population regardless of their subgroup membership. He discusses five widely used item bias detection procedures: analysis of variance, transformed item difficulties, chi square, item characteristic curve, and distractor response.

The presentation in this monograph assumes knowledge of elementary statistical concepts and techniques. The discussion of the use of analysis of variance procedures to detect bias, for example, builds on a presumed base of knowledge of variance partitioning in straightforward ANOVA procedures. The reader's background in these topics, however, may be largely intuitive and conceptual rather than detailed. Certainly a broad background in theoretical statistics is not required to follow Dr. Osterlind's presentation, which generally makes minimal use of formal notation and algebraic manipulations. *Test Item Bias* contains ample charts and examples drawn largely from educational psychology. Rather than presenting detailed examples, Dr. Osterlind has used them largely to illustrate general points or to provide simple examples of the techniques he is presented herein.

Test Item Bias is most directly relevent for educational psychologists and researchers engaged in practical rather than theoretical work. It is clearly a "how to" manual for those of us interested in developing achievement or ability tests that are as "fair" as possible, and it suggests several avenues open to researchers to help ensure that items possessing unfair biases will be detected and replaced by items that are less likely to contain such biases. Dr. Osterlind's experience as research director for the Oakland Unified School District has provided him with ample experience in dealing with these issues.

—John L. Sullivan
Series Co-Editor

TEST ITEM BIAS

STEVEN J. OSTERLIND
Oakland, California,
Unified School District

1. INTRODUCTION

What This Monograph Is About

The subject of this monograph is test item bias; it is a discussion of appropriate statistical procedures to explore the psychometric properties of bias in standardized test items. The primary objective is to convey to the reader an understanding of the term "item bias" and to provide an introduction to practical techniques that may be used in its detection and correction. The focus of attention is exclusively on technical criteria for item bias that is internal to the test instrument. Social consequences of test use and predictive validity for the total test, as well as fairness of tests and other concerns of external validity, are not addressed here. There are a number of technical criteria for internal bias for test items as well as statistical methods for detecting it. This monograph presents an introduction to such technical criteria for item bias and five biased item detection strategies.

The biased item investigation strategies described represent the most broadly based spectrum of practical alternative procedures available today. Each technique is presented in a manner that will allow the reader to duplicate the procedure with original data on test scores. Accompanying all five descriptions of strategies is a discussion of various test hypotheses. Circumstances in which they may be appropriately applied are also considered.

The need for such a work is self-evident. In the field of tests and measurement the word bias has become an almost empty pejorative, meaning anything bad, bigoted, racist, or suppressive. Bias is the focus of the accusation that tests are unfair, inconstant, contaminated by extraneous factors, and subject to misuse and abuse. But what is really meant by the accusation that tests are biased? Are these charges valid?

There are at least two approaches that one may take to answer these questions. One approach is to examine the use to which test scores may be put. Selection of applicants to schools, jobs, and a variety of programs and services often rests to large degree on test scores. This approach requires the comparison of test results for particular groups against some outside criterion: For example, how many applicants from each group were accepted to the program? (There are a number of bias-in-selection models available to guide one in making such comparisons and although this monograph does not describe them specifically, I shall have more to say about them shortly.)

An alternative route to understanding the accusation that tests are biased is to examine the test items themselves in the absence of an outside criterion. For the legitimate use of tests, it is crucial that all examinees be assured of equity in test items as far as their achievement or ability may be reliably assessed. Tests should be constructed so that when an inequality exists between groups' test scores, the disparity is due primarily to differences in whatever it is the test purports to measure. By the detection and elimination of biased items, tests can be constructed to this standard. This monograph presents several statistical models for examining bias in test items without reference to an outside criterion.

This monograph is also intended to meet the existing need to identify, organize, and synthesize from a wide variety of sources the most developed and practical strategies for investigating internal bias in standardized tests. Because the field of internal test item bias is so young, it is understandable that little prior organization exists. The psychometrics appropriate for this kind of study are a recent development, and computers (also a comparatively recent development) are necessary for most of them. I have accumulated all of the information I could find on how one might expect test items to behave psychometrically when different subgroups of a population are compared. The unique contribution of this monograph is that it gathers in one source all of the major strategies for investigating item bias.

How This Monograph Is Organized

The monograph contains two parts. This chapter presents precursory information to Chapters 2 through 6, the heart of the monograph. In this chapter I will introduce the topic of item bias in tests, synthesize some opinions about bias, and present a commonly accepted technical definition for bias in psychological testing. The discussion will be brief, only relating the information necessary to understand the strategies presented in the following chapters. A more detailed examination of the concept of bias in some intelligence and achievement tests is offered in two recent books: *Ability Testing: Uses, Consequences and Controversies, Parts I and II* (National Research Council, Committee on Ability Testing, 1982) and *Bias In Mental Testing* (Jensen, 1980). After the introduction I will describe some essential assumptions and terms and offer a very brief preview of each of the five biased item detection strategies discussed in this monograph. The following chapters explore in separate sections each of the five biased item detection strategies.

The format for presentation of each procedure is uniform. First is a description of the item investigation strategy and its function; following this is a discussion of the hypotheses that may be interrogated by the approach; next the statistics are described; finally, there is mention of appropriate use of the technique and inherent limitations. In each instance I will draw examples of the techniques from real studies. In a concluding chapter I will summarize the essential points for each technique described as well as provide a chart for comparing the methodologies.

I assume that the reader will have some introductory background in statistics and testing methodology. Familiarity with beginning algebra will also be helpful. While examples with actual data sets will be presented, the description of the techniques will involve commonly used statistical models. The statistical models themselves are not explained here; their descriptions are readily available from other monographs in this series or from a wide variety of introductory statistical texts (e.g., Lord and Novick, 1974; Marascuilo, 1971; Nunnally, 1978; Winer, 1962).

The issues involved in test item bias are complex, and before we begin, the reader will need to understand clearly what is and what is not included in a discussion of test item bias.

As mentioned earlier, criteria for the examination of bias in test items may be *external* or *internal* to the test instrument itself. External bias is the degree to which test scores may manifest a correlational relationship with variables independent of the test. A frequently cited example of the nature of this correlational relationship is the association of Scholastic Aptitude Test (SAT) scores with college grade point average. The whole test, rather than individual test items, is usually of concern in external bias. Issues involved in external bais are construct validity for the total test and predictive validity. Social consequences of test use as well as fairness in tests and models for selection criteria are examples of external bias issues. The *Journal of Educational Measurement* devoted an entire issue (Spring 1976) to external bias. Two of the articles are particularly excellent discussions of external bias topics: "Equity in Selection—Where Psychometrics and Political Philosophy Meet" (Lee J. Cronbach) and "An Evaluation of Some Models for Culture Fair Selection" (Nancy S. Peterson and Melvin R. Novick). External bias is not treated in any way in this monograph.

Internal bias concerns the psychometric properties of test items themselves. It may be considered a particular kind of item analysis aimed at answering the question: When subjected to particular statistical tests, do standardized test items behave in an identical manner for different subgroups drawn from the same population? The procedures described in this monograph are techniques to determine the degree of internal bias for items under a given hypothesis.

One further point regarding criteria for bias needs to be mentioned. Bias in psychological tests is a wide-ranging issues, and this monograph explores only one rather limited aspect of bias (i.e., internal bias for test items). The criterion for bias described will be adequate for our purposes, but it is certainly not exhaustive of the topic. One description of the widely disparate components of test bias is given by Flaugher (1978). The interested reader wishing to explore the general topic further is referred to this fine article as well as to the references cited at the end of this monograph for a more comprehensive look at bias issues in psychological tests.

What Is Bias?

The term "bias," when used to describe mental tests and other measurements, has a specific and unique meaning. Bias is defined as a systematic error in the measurement process. It affects all measurements in the same way, changing measurement—sometimes increasing it and other times decreasing it. The term is conceptually distinct and operationally different from the concepts of fairness, equality, prejudice, or preference or any of the other connotations sometimes associated with its use in popular speech. Bias, then, is a technical term and denotes nothing more or less than the consistent distortion of a statistic. Throughout this monograph bias will be used strictly in the technical sense; no other meaning is implied nor should any be inferred.

Let us look at what is meant by the operational definition of bias, the "systematic distortion of a statistic." It may be easiest to understand this notion of bias through an example. Official measurements in the U.S. Bureau of Standards are a combination of measurements between the K_{20} and the kilogram. It has been empirically determined that these two measures are not precisely equal, the K_{20} is estimated to be 19 parts in a billion lighter than the kilogram. Therefore, all measurements at the bureau done by K_{20} are systematically off (or biased) by this very small amount. Since many measurements require extreme accuracy, the bureau compensates for this measurement bias by revising K_{20} measurements up by 19 parts in a billion. But regardless of compensating remedies, the example shows a systematic error in measurement—or bias.

In test items, bias is also considered the presence of a systematic error in measurement. Items are judged relatively more or less difficult for a particular subgroup by comparison with the performance(s) of another subgroup or groups drawn from the same population. Test items are interrogated by the various item bias detection techniques available in an effort to determine whether or not they conform to a given set of psychometric rules in the same way for all persons in a population, regardless of any subgroup membership within that population (e.g., ethnicity, sex).

The concern of bias in psychological tests is construct validity for items, that is, the extent to which a test item (or set of items) may be said to measure a single, definable theoretical construct or trait. When items have the same construct validity for all examinees in a population, examinees of comparable ability should have the same chance of getting the item correct. In test theory, the chance of an examinee correctly responding to an item is termed the *probability of success*. Internal bias may be identified by comparing probabilities of success for examinees from different subgroups of the same population. A test item is said to be *unbiased* when the probability for success on the item is the same for equally able examinees of the same population regardless of their subgroup group membership.

This criterion is the standard against which we shall examine specific psychometric properties of test items by a variety of techniques. Each of the biased item detection approaches presented in this monograph uses a slightly different strategy toward examining bias, but our criterion will remain unchanged throughout. This will enable us to work through a variety of perspectives toward bias on a common standard.

One naive but widely held notion of bias should be quickly dispelled. Virtually everyone working in the field of test item bias agrees on this point. Bias is not the mere presence of a score difference between two groups. Were this true, every item would be "biased" against or in favor of one group or another and "bias" could be repeatedly inferred by merely redefining the groups. The logic of this argument would have every item "biased" for or against one or another ethnic group, or one sex, or tall persons, or any other variable that one could name. This thinking confuses the issue of item bias with any number of irrelevant variables such as curricular validity of the instrument, equal opportunity to subject materials, violations of standardization of testing environment, and the like. An example may help to illustrate the point.

At a local university the track team takes frequent running excursions through the town. Suppose all students at the university were asked a question regarding identification of street location within the city limits. Obviously (other things equal) due to their increased familiarity with the streets, members of the track team would answer the question correctly more often than would other students. But does this mean the question is biased? Not necessarily; in fact, it may reveal differences in subject matter awareness (in this case, familiarity with street names), and thus is an appropriate measure. Still the point remains, from the information given (only that track team members answered the question correctly more often than did other students), we cannot conclude anything about bias one way or the other. An empirical examination of psychometric properties of the item by one or more of the techniques presented in Chapters 2 through 6 is needed to more fully answer the question.

Assumptions and Terms

One assumption of test theory is especially important in item bias work. It is the assumption that test items are intended to measure only a single attribute or skill for examinees. This is called *unidimensionality* for items and is a commonly accepted assumption for item development by test constructors. Without the assumption of unidimensionality, the interpretation of item responses is profoundly complex. We shall presume unidimensionality for all items interrogated by any of the bias detection strategies. When the assumption holds true, the pattern of responses to items by subgroups drawn from the same population is expected to be similar, regardless of differences in overall ability of the subgroups. More able examinees will generally answer correctly more items and more difficult items and will guess at answers fewer times than will students who are less able in the measured trait or attribute. When this is not the case, different attributes are likely to be measured, and the unidimensionality assumption is violated. Whenever the assumption for unidimensionality of items is suspected to be different across groups, the question of item bias should be investigated.

Two terms regularly used in tests and measurement are item *difficulty* and item *discrimination*. These terms are especially important in test item bias work, and we shall rely on them frequently throughout this monograph. They are not identical, although their definitions overlap. The difficulty of an item is defined operationally as the proportion of examinees in a given population (or subpopulation) who were successful on the item (i.e., answered correctly). The item difficulty is denoted as the p value, and I use this symbol throughout this monograph. As an example, suppose a given test question was administered to 100 examinees and 65 of them answered correctly. The p value is .65 (i.e., 65/100). Although p value is the most common, other item difficulty indices are also used in some test item bias investigations. These indices will be discussed as they occur.

Item *discrimination* is somewhat more difficult to understand than is item difficulty. Item discrimination refers to the degree to which an item correctly differentiates examinees in whatever behavior it is that the test measures. Item discrimination is usually considered as a given item against the total score on the test itself. Thus an item that discriminates well is one in which there is a separation (in terms of p values) of high achievers (typically, the top 27% of examinees) from low achievers (again, typically, the lowest 27% of examinees). For example, consider two items on a test, items 1 and 2. Suppose that for item 1 the top group of achievers had a p value of .86 compared to the low achiever's p value of .41. This item discriminates well between high and low achievers. Suppose again that for item 2 the high achievers had a p value of .75, while the bottom group of achievers obtained a p value of .72. This item discriminates very little between the top and bottom groups of achievers.

Sometimes it is convenient to note the difference in p values between the groups as a single index. To continue the example from above, for item 1 the item discrimination index is .45 (.86 – .41); for item 2 it is .03 (.75 – .72).

Item discrimination is a positive feature of tests. It enables one to reliably infer differences among examinees. Without it tests generally would be useless. A test with a zero discrimination index would not reveal anything about the examinees. When particular items discriminate differently among individuals or groups of the same ability then the suspicion of bias is raised. Item discrimination plays an important part in each of the biased item detection strategies discussed in this monograph.

Strategies Preview

The five procedures for detecting possible bias in test items described in this monograph are each named by similarity with concomitant statistical tests. They are: analysis of variance (ANOVA), transformed item difficulties (TID), chi square (χ^2), item characteristic curve (ICC), and distractor response analysis (distractor). It should be kept in mind that each of these strategies represents a range of approaches to ferret out the degree of bias that may be present in specific test items. None is a single technique; rather, each represents a family of routes to follow. Nor are the strategies independent of each other; they overlap and build upon one another, as often as not attempting to address weaknesses in alternative strategies. With this in mind, it becomes increasingly important to understand the assumptions underlying each strategy as well as appropriate hypotheses. These will be clearly discussed in the respective chapters of the monograph, and the reader should study these chapters thoroughly before attempting the use of the statistics of a given strategy.

Analysis of variance (ANOVA) strategy. In the ANOVA approach to the detection of biased items, two or more groups sampled from the same population are given a common test, and the resultant variations in individual item scores are interrogated with an analysis of variance design. It is the interaction of groups $\times$ items, rather than simple main effects, that is the principal focus for attention. The interaction contrast for every item within each group forms the criterion on which judgments about item bias may be made.

Transformed item difficulties (TID). In this approach to detecting and correcting test item bias, bias is considered to be a characteristic inherent in all test items, and the degree to which individual test items exhibit this property is the focus of attention. Conceptually, the TID approach is very similar to the ANOVA strategy for biased item detection: relative item difficulties for two or more groups' performances on a set of test questions covering a single skill or mental construct are revealed by the interaction of groups with items. But beyond merely describing the groups × items interaction, as it is done by ANOVA, the TID strategy seeks to identify particular biased test items by their degree of aberrance. It is easily seen that TID is sometimes thought of as a post hoc procedure to the ANOVA strategy.

Chi square (χ^2). This approach to the identification of test item bias examines the likelihood—or probability—of correctly responding to an item for test takers from different groups with the same ability levels. An item is considered unbiased when all persons of a given ability level have an equal probability of correctly answering an item regardless of anyone's group membership as to ethnicity, sex, age, or other discrete subpopulation. The essential strategy of this technique is to remove biased item identification from the dependency upon the groups × items interaction as the arbiter of bias, the case for ANOVA and TID. Instead, with χ^2 strategy, the proportion of responses within ability categories for two groups diverse in some given criterion variable is examined.

The technique is of the goodness-of-fit type in that from the null hypothesis of no difference a significance test is made between an expected number of examinee responses in a particular ability level category and the actual number that was observed to respond in that category. Thus the χ^2 approach to test item bias is sensitive to within-groups' item discrimination in addition to giving attention to differences between groups in item difficulty levels.

Item characteristic curve (ICC). Certainly these approaches are the most elegant of all the models discussed to tease out test item bias. ICC techniques are also difficult to understand conceptually and extremely complex procedurally. Computer processing of data is the only practical way the ICC methods may be exploited. Because the procedures are technically complex and require advanced background in statistics for a thorough understanding, we shall explore this method more fully than any of the other procedures described. In cursory preview terms, however, probabilities of getting an item correct for each of two groups are compared. Item characteristic curves graphically display the probability function. The overall notion is that the item characteristic curves generated for each of two groups should be alike for an item to be considered unbiased.

Distractor response analysis (distractor). This is the final test item bias procedure to be discussed. Examining the incorrect alternatives to a test item—usually termed *distractors* but sometimes called question *foils*—for differences in patterns of response among different subgroups of a population is the essential strategy of the distractor response analysis technique. The function of Distractor is to determine the significance of the differences among two or more groups' response frequencies in the discrete categories of question distractors. If a significance test reveals that two or more groups distinguished by some criterion are in fact differentially attracted to a test items' distractors, the null hypothesis (of no difference in the groups' relative frequencies for distractors) may be rejected and bias is inferred to be present.

Quick but Incomplete Methods

A quick and very simple procedure to give one a preliminary idea of the degree of bias in a set of test items is to compare the rankings item difficulty values between two groups. The difficulty index used most often for this kind of comparison is the item p value for each group. The p value rankings for each group should be placed side by side to facilitate comparisons, as in the example in Table 1. The suspicion of bias is raised for any item that deviates sharply from the general pattern of rankings.

Suppose the data for a five-item test are distributed as shown in Table 1. Notice in Table 1 that item 2 is the easiest for both groups regardless of the fact that a substantially higher percentage of examinees in Group I got the item correct than did examinees in Group II (i.e., $P_I = .93$ and $P_{II} = .81$). However, the pattern is not continued for item 4. This item is only second in difficulty ranking for Group I, but it is the most difficult of all the items for Group II. Thus the suspicion is raised

TABLE 1
Rank Order of Item Difficulty for a Hypothetical Test

Item	Rank Order for Group I (p value)	Rank Order for Group II (p value)
1	3rd (p = .62)	2nd (p = .64)
2	1st (p = .93)	1st (p = .81)
3	4th (p = .55)	3rd (p = .51)
4	2nd (p = .71)	5th (p = .19)
5	5th (p = .28)	4th (p = .38)

$\rho = .40$.

that item 4 does not behave similarily between the two groups. Bias may be present in the item to a degree that consistently underestimates the performance of Group II. All other items appear to rank in a pattern similar for both groups, and no other item is suspected of aberrance.

A rank order correlation coefficient (ρ) between the two sets of values can be computed for further confirmation of aberrance. For correlations of this kind one would look for rank order correlation coefficients of .90 or higher to judge for similarity in rankings of item difficulty values between groups. In the example, the coefficient of correlation is .40. This comparatively low level of correlation between the rankings of item difficulty supports our suspicion of bias by this method. (Admittedly, the coefficient of correlation in this illustration may be distorted by the very small numbers of test items.)

It should be clearly understood, however, that comparing the rank order of item difficulty indices between groups is an incomplete strategy for concluding bias in test items. It is, nevertheless, a useful tool as an early indication of whether or not particular items behave differently between groups.

There is another approach to exploring bias in items in psychological tests that has superficial appeal, but it is not recommended. This approach uses factor analysis. Factor analysis makes efforts to explain the construct validity of the measure, that is, what factors lie behind the test performance. The concept investigated by the procedure is that the test score variance is composed of the same theoretical constructs, or factors, for different groups. When this is not the case it may be inferred that different theoretical constructs are at work for each group and items contributing to these differences may be ipso facto biased. The assumptions to the approach lie more in the property being measured than in the test itself.

The reasons why factor analysis is not recommended in test item bias work, despite its conceptual appeal, are fundamental. First of all, no rationale exists for deciding which factors could legitimately be extracted, and there is no appropriate statistical test available to compare the factor loadings. Another reason it is not recommended in bias investigations is that in computations the scores of one group are regressed onto those of another, and no logical rationale exists for deciding which group to select for the regression. For these reasons, then, factor analysis is not recommended in test item bias work.

New Territory

Studies of bias in standardized tests are certainly not a recent phenomenon. Binet and Simon introduced one early version of their intelligence test in 1905 and almost immediately noticed group differences between scores from children of Parisian working-class homes and those of children from a higher social status. Later versions of their intelligence tests attempted to control this "cultural bias" by eliminating items they believed revealed social class differences. And in 1951 Chicago psychologist Kenneth Eells produced a classic study of cultural bias in test items and even explicated a methodology for investigation of differences in IQ among various cultural groups.

What might be termed the modern era of investigation into item bias—that is, strategies involving sophisticated statistics and usually requiring computers to handle the elaborate calculations—can be dated to an article titled "An Investigation of Item Bias," which appeared in the respected journal of psychometrics, *Educational and Psychological Measurement* (Cleary and Hilton, 1968). This article detailed a study of Preliminary Scholastic Aptitude Test (PSAT) items by the ANOVA technique for detection of test item bias. Its significance lies in the fact that this study was the progenitor of rapid and substantial advances in examining the degree of bias within items from a purely statistical point of view. Despite methodological shortcomings the ANOVA strategy continues to be widely practiced in item bias studies today.

Partly in response to the flaws of ANOVA, the Educational Testing Service (ETS) developed an alternative procedure for examining items called transformed item difficulties (Angoff, 1972; Angoff and Ford,

1973). This approach also holds popularity today as a preliminary method for screening items during development of new tests.

Green and Draper (1972) proposed early on the use of item means and item test correlations as a strategy for determining the presence or absence of content bias in achievement tests. Serious shortcomings of this approach soon became evident (see Hunter, 1975), and it is not now recommended.

The next big advancement in test item bias methodology was proposed by Janice Scheuneman (1979) of ETS. This procedure was originally called the chi-square approach because of its reliance on an original statistic that superficially looked very much like a traditional chi-square procedure. However, the approach was widely criticized for its shortcomings (see Baker, 1981; Marascuilo and Slaughter, 1981a). Marascuilo, a theoretical statistician working at University of California, Berkeley, developed a series of item bias procedures that overcome some of the shortcomings of the Scheuneman technique and are more nearly related to a true chi-square statistic. Marascuilo's chi-square strategies supersede Scheuneman's earlier work.

Meanwhile, there was significant and prodigious work being done in item response theory (also called latent trait theory) by a variety of researchers and statisticians. Its applicability to investigations of bias within test items soon became evident (see Lord, 1977a, 1977b). A great deal of the work on test item bias being done today by researchers, testing companies, and others utilizes item response theory. As already mentioned, we will explore this approach thoroughly.

These developments in item bias theory are mentioned to give a little background into how we got where we are today. It is not intended to be a historical account. Such an account is available, however, to the interested reader in Diamond (1981).

One should note the very recent dates and development of these methodologies. This field certainly is young. Also, and it is important to realize, the wide availability of sophisticated computer programs makes all of the techniques described, even the most complex, practical for application by researchers today. Inevitably, future developments into the psychometric properties of these statistical procedures will add much to their power and integrity. These will be welcome developments.

A final note is necessary before beginning the discussion of the several bias detection strategies. Every attempt has been made to point out both the strengths and limitations of each procedure as well as to specify situations in which one or another (or all or none) of the techniques may be appropriately used. Still, caution should be exercised before making inferential judgments about the degree of bias or lack of bias in specific test items. While addressing the heart of the matter in test item bias, construct validity for test items, the APA *Standards for Educational and Psychological Tests* (1974) notes, "Evidence of construct validity is not found in a single study; rather, judgments . . . are based upon the accumulation of research results." These biased item detection strategies should be used in conjunction with judgmental approaches and external evidence, as well as with other indicators of bias in tests before decisions regarding specific items or tests become final. Now, on to the techniques themselves.

2. ANALYSIS OF VARIANCE

We begin our discussion of several approaches for seeking out item bias in psychological tests with the analysis of variance strategy (ANOVA). In the ANOVA approach to the detection of biased items two or more groups sampled from the same population are given a common test and the resultant variations in individual item scores are interrogated with an analysis of variance design. It is the interaction of groups $\times$ items, rather than simple main effects, that is the principal focus of attention. The interaction contrast for every item within each group forms the criterion on which judgments about item bias may be made.

Analysis of variance as a statistical technique is powerful and useful in many research and evaluation settings, but ANOVA as a bias detection strategy is flawed and cumbersome in its application. As we shall see several other strategies for unearthing test item bias may be more convenient, appropriate, or uncluttered with the deficiencies and flaws that beset ANOVA methodology when used for this purpose. Why then, one may ask, begin a presentation of various test bias detection techniques with one so fraught with limitations and imperfections? There are at least three reasons for doing so.

First of all, despite defects and shortcomings ANOVA presents several attractive features useful to learning about test bias. Of paramount importance is the group $\times$ items interaction effect as revealed by analysis of variance. This component of the statistic is fundamental to all test item bias methodologies as presently practiced. Bias detection techniques are either based on the assumption of this effect as a reliable and valid indicator of inherent bias in test items, or the groups × items bias indicator assumption is soundly criticized and scrupulously advoided. An appreciation of the role of ANOVA in test item bias methodology is therefore a requisite for an understanding of the various approaches in any contemplated item bias investigation.

An additional reason to begin our discussion with ANOVA is its historical importance as a model in test item bias methodology. Early work in the field included several seminal ANOVA item bias studies. We shall examine some of these studies and their relevance for researchers today. Finally, despite its shortcomings the use of ANOVA in test item bias studies is still comparatively popular. Its widespread use may persist in part because many persons are familiar with the analysis of variance statistic.

It was noted earlier that items that measure a different trait or attribute for subgroups drawn from the same population violate the assumption of unidimensionality of items. Items lacking unidimensionality across subgroups will likely exhibit varying degrees of difficulty regardless of the groups' overall ability level difference. The groups × items interaction of analysis of variance procedures will reveal this effect of different levels of difficulty between or among groups. And when ability levels are held constant, test items that are more or less difficult for examinees of one group than for members of another group do not meet our criterion for bias; namely, a test item is said to be unbiased when the difficulty level (more technically termed "probability for success") on a test item is the same for equally able examinees of the same population regardless of their subgroup membership. Hence, bias is inferred whenever a significant groups × items interaction is observed in the analysis of variance statistic.

In the ANOVA procedure, the interaction effects for each group are plotted on a bivariate graph, one group on each axis, which visually reflects the results of the analysis of variance. Originally in the technique, simply "eyeballing" the plotted interactions allowed for a simple interpretation: Conclude bias for the items with pronounced values. But in most item bias investigations today, at least one of a variety of alternative post hoc procedures is generally used to identify individual aberrant items.

To see how the ANOVA procedure works in practice, let us construct some graphs displaying the groups × items interaction. The graphs themselves are easily constructed. For all tested items the percentage of examinees in each of two groups who got a given item

22

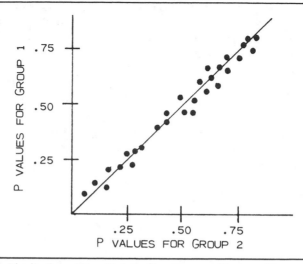

Figure 1: Distribution of Item Plots for Two Groups with $r_{xy} = .98$

correct (p value) is calculated. The p values of a given item for the two groups become the coordinates for plotting the item on the axes of a bivariate graph. The p values for one group are plotted along the abscissa (i.e., x or horizontal axis) and those for the other group are plotted on the ordinate (i.e., y or vertical axis). From the point of origin on the graph (i.e., x = 0, y = 0) a 45-degree line may be drawn. Items with identical p values for both groups will fall exactly on the line; items easier or more difficult for one group than for the other will fall away from the line.

Figures 1 and 2 display examples of item plots of the interactions for test items with two groups. The p values for the groups are plotted in the manner described. If the groups are homogenous to one another in the attribute measured, the plotted points will form a long narrow ellipse, as in Figure 1. Typically, with two similar groups the p values for both groups produce a very high correlation (e.g., $r_{xy} = .98$ or higher).

But this condition seldom exists in reality. Much more common is the situation in which the groups are heterogeneous to each other in the ability measured and are not equally dispersed. Consider Figure 2, in which p values are plotted for two divergent groups. Here the pattern of plotted item difficulty indices is not linear but curvilinear and forms an open ellipse. The items are obviously more difficult for Group 1 than

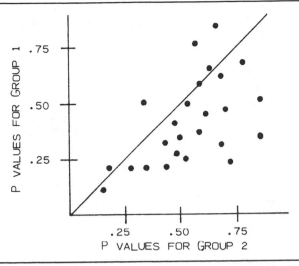

Figure 2: Distribution of Item Plots for Two Groups with $r_{xy} = .90$

they are for Group 2. Correlations between the groups may be as low as .90 or even lower. If the points were randomly dispersed forming a circle pattern the correlation would, of course, be zero. The presumption is that the groups × items interaction contributed to the less than perfect correlation, and this may be construed as an indication of test item bias. Let us examine this presumption.

The Theory

Recall that analysis of variance is a method for analyzing variance (i.e., variation in a set of measurements) into a number of additive components that together equal the total score variance. The components of the total variance are the between-groups variance, the within-groups variance, and an error variance. This may be stated as:

$$V_t = V_b + V_w + V_e \qquad [1]$$

The interrogation of the variance components is the analysis of variance strategy. But in the ANOVA procedure the focus of attention is solely on the interaction of groups × items; other variance components are not directly considered by this biased item detection technique. Therefore, we must express the variance in terms that allow for an examination of just the interaction of items with groups.

Variance may be expressed mathematically as the square of the standard deviation of a set of values, $V = \sigma^2$. The total score variance for a given item i, and a particular group j, at a response level, either correct or incorrect, k, may be represented as σ_{ijk}^2. Thus the additive components of the total score variance may be rewritten as:

$$\sigma_{ijk}^2 = \sigma_i^2 + \sigma_j^2 + \sigma_{ij}^2 + \sigma_{k(ij)}^2 \qquad [2]$$

That is, the total score variance equals the sum of the variance due to items, the variance due to groups, the variance of the interaction of items with groups, and an error variance. With the groups $\times$ items interaction variance expressed in mathematical terms, we are now able to present an appropriate hypothesis for testing by analysis of variance. Specifically, the hypothesis of interest by the ANOVA strategy is:

$$H_0: \sigma_{ij}^2 = 0$$

against the alternative:

$$H_1: \sigma_{ij}^2 \neq 0$$

The null hypothesis states that there is no interaction between items i and groups j. The usual analysis of variance statistic will test the adequacy of this hypothesis. The independent variables for manipulation are always group membership and items; the dependent variable is the number of individuals responding correctly. Of course, group membership as a description for an independent variable merely means to describe which groups are to be considered in the investigation (e.g., various ethnic heritage groups, the two sexes) and not to imply one may transfer or be randomly assigned to arbitrarily named groups.

If in the ANOVA statistic no significant relationship exists between the independent variables and the dependent variable (as revealed by an F value not sufficiently large to reject the null hypothesis), it is as though the numbers used for the test were randomly chosen from appropriate groups, and consequently the groups' scores have a random mean and no bias for items is inferred. However, if the F test in the ANOVA design does show the means to be significantly different, a relation exists between the groups' membership and items, and the number of individuals responding correctly. Bias for items is inferred by the contribution of group membership to item scores and is said to be a contributing factor to this portion of the score variance.

Although this supposition is held to be true in the ANOVA approach, it is nevertheless troublesome. The fact that test item bias by ANOVA is attributed only to a significant interaction confounds what may well be the consequences of several variance sources, some of which do not constitute item bias at all. Of course, the groups and the items can individually account for a large portion of the total score variance, but other sources may also contribute. For example, item score variance could be attributed to differences in item difficulty as some items may be more difficult than others. Or the differences may be due to the groups, where one group may be more able in the attribute measured than the other; or it may be within groups, where subjects differ in ability. This characteristic of ANOVA to specify only that variance components exist in interaction to a significant degree and not partition out the source of the variance is one of its most criticized shortcomings (see Hunter, 1975).

Keep in mind, however, that test item bias in the ANOVA strategy is defined as a significant groups × items interaction in the sense that items exist that can be *relatively* more difficult for members of one group than for those of another. The relative character of item bias will be explored further in the discussion of the transformed item difficulty approach to detecting test item bias, a procedure closely allied with ANOVA bias methods.

Post Hoc Procedures

Putting aside the problems discussed above for a moment, however, when a significant groups × items interaction is revealed by ANOVA methods, a follow-up procedure should be used to identify which, if any, particular items contributed inordinately to the interaction. Logically, such a post hoc procedure should be a series of comparisons among the several means considered in the ANOVA. Either of two statistical methods is usually employed to make several comparisons among means: Tukey's method of multiple pairwise contrasts or Scheffe's method of multiple comparisons. But neither of these post hoc procedures is recommended in test item bias work. Tukey's test requires equal sample sizes among groups, a situation rarely achieved in real-world research for test investigation settings. Some researchers suggest that sample sizes be artifically changed by discarding some number of randomly chosen subjects from the larger group to achieve equal numbers, but this is not recommended because it threatens the integrity of the ANOVA assumption of independence of groups. Another reason why Tukey's post hoc procedure may be inappropriate is that it is much too conservative for practical work in test item bias investigations. The same can also be said for Scheffe's method.

Other post hoc procedures are available, however. The path to biased item detection known as transformed item difficulties (TID) is certainly a logical choice for a post hoc procedure when by ANOVA the overall F ratio is statistically significant. In the TID approach an index of item difficulty (typically p values) is obtained for tested items for each of two groups as was done for ANOVA. But with TID the item difficulties are converted, or transformed, to a normal deviate, usually delta (Δ), and then plotted on a graph for visual inspection. When individual item difficulty indices are normalized, identifying particular items for aberrance is relatively simple. Each item is compared with all other items. A major axis line is fitted to the plotted points, and the further away from this line any item plot falls, the greater the degree of bias that is presumed to exist for that item. The TID approach, which is discussed fully in the next chapter, is a common follow-up procedure to ANOVA in test item bias work.

Problems and Limitations

With the ANOVA methods if the null hypothesis of no significant interaction effect of groups $\times$ items is rejected, the suspicion of bias is raised. And by post hoc procedures, as the items that contributed differentially to the interaction are identified, the suspicion of bias is particularized to specific test items. From this it can be concluded that some kind of bias does exist to some degree within the test. But the converse does not stand. That is, bias cannot be wholly dismissed as nonexistent nor can it be concluded that the test is free of bias merely because the null hypotheses is not rejected.

Earlier it was mentioned that the groups $\times$ items interaction can occur in tests merely as a function of differences in overall group performance or by differing ability levels. This presents a serious dilemma for users of ANOVA methodology, for they must face the decision of whether or not to conclude a test contains bias by the very suspect criterion of no significant groups × item interaction. One way to alleviate partially this concern is to employ a selection rule for identifying group membership in such a way that each group selected has a range of achievement within it but also equal distribution of raw scores among groups. Blocking groups on instructional level may be a reasonable criterion for such a selection rule (Plake, 1981). But even this alternative can be limited in real-world bias studies due to the typically small sample of numbers of ethnic heritage minority students in most tested populations; still, it does have some intrinsic appeal.

A final but less serious problem rests with the overall alpha level used for significance testing in the post hoc analysis. This alpha level can become inflated as the number of test items increases. The result is a threat to commit a high rate of Type I errors.

Research Examples

Several studies of test item bias using ANOVA methodology will be mentioned briefly. The idea here is to convey a feeling for the contexts and purposes in which ANOVA is an appropriate route rather than to describe completely various studies.

One early and seminal study to employ the analysis of variance design to investigate test item bias was conducted as a result of concern expressed by the College Entrance Examination Board about the appropriateness of the Scholastic Aptitude Test (SAT) and the Preliminary Scholastic Aptitude Test (PSAT) for some subgroups of the population, particularly Black examinees (Cleary and Hilton, 1968). In the study a three-factor analysis of variance design was used. The first factor considered in the design was ethnic heritage of examinees; the second factor, socioeconomic status (SES), was considered fixed and nested within race. A third factor was considered as random: items. It was not assumed that SES levels were comparable in the two ethnic heritage groups. Also, the study considered SES levels and race as fixed effects. The principal hypothesis under test was that there is no interaction between items and race.

Few of the tested effects and none of the interaction effects were found to be significant. When major components of the variance were estimated, only a small percentage of the total variance was contributed by the within subjects items × race interaction. It was concluded that for practical purposes the PSAT was not biased for the groups studied.

An even earlier study of psychometric evidence for bias in tests, conducted in 1963, also used ANOVA methodology but with the arcsine transformation for expressing item difficulties (Cardall and Coffman, 1964). Here, a highly significant groups × items interaction was found for both the verbal and mathematical subtests of the SAT. The hypothesis of no interaction of groups × items was rejected for both the verbal and mathematical items. The authors conjectured that the relative difficulty of items changes from group to group to a greater extent than one would expect as a result of random sampling. They attempted to verify this speculation by preparing for analysis a table of correlations of item difficulty among groups. They reasoned that those instances in which the groups × items interaction effect was statistically significant would have relatively low coefficients of correlation. Their reasoning was supported by the correlational data: The lower the correlation, the higher the interaction.

Thus it can be seen that the ANOVA approach is widely used in pointing out initial suspicion of bias, but by itself, the groups × items interaction is an incomplete criterion on which to conclude bias for test items. The post hoc procedures, as well as other confirming analyses, become important for a more complete look at bias.

3. TRANSFORMED ITEM DIFFICULTIES

In the approach to detecting and correcting test item bias known as transformed item difficulties (TID), bias is considered to be a characteristic inherent in all test items, and the degree to which individual test items exhibit this property is the focus of attention. Conceptually, the TID approach is very similar to the ANOVA strategy for biased item detection: Relative item difficulties for two or more groups' performances on a set of test questions covering a single skill or mental construct are revealed by the interaction of groups with items. But beyond merely describing the groups × items interaction, as was done by ANOVA, the TID strategy seeks to identify particular biased test items by their degree of aberrance.

Hence, bias as investigated with the TID approach is a *relative* standard; an item is considered biased when it is comparatively more difficult to answer correctly for one group than it is for the other. The assimption is that bias is indicated by a signficant group difference in the relative difficulty of the item rather than by a group difference in the means, or standard deviations, of the p values or some other item difficulty index. It is easily seen that TID is sometimes thought of as a post hoc procedure to the ANOVA strategy.

Advantages

The TID approach offers a number of advantages over many other techniques for unearthing biased items. First of all, and importantly, the TID approach is conceptually straightforward. The underlying logic is simply to test if different groups interact with a set of test items in the same way. If test items do interact in the same way with different subgroups of a population, the items' variations of difficulty are approximately the same among equally able individuals for either group regardless of whether or not the overall means between the groups are the same size. When this is not the case it may be inferred that the particular items manifest different kinds of responses from each group, and bias is concluded for those items. As was true with the ANOVA strategy, in the TID approach the integrity of the assumption of unidimensionality for items between different groups must be maintained.

Another advantage of the TID methodology is that the procedures for the technique provide for graphing item difficulties in a manner that allows for visual inspection of relative degrees of item bias. The visual presentation of the data doubtless adds to its popular appeal, particularly among laypersons.

Also, TIDs, by virtue of their comparative simplicity, are adaptable to a variety of research settings. And finally, TIDs allow for equating scores or standardizing and equating item difficulties. This purpose may be served by the TID approach because of its historical roots in a method of absolute scaling (see Thurstone, 1925).

Tested Hypothesis

It is important to understand the exact nature of how variables may be related for significance testing by TID methodology. The hypothesis under test by this strategy is not solely the presence or absence of groups $\times$ items interaction, as was the case with ANOVA procedures. With TIDs the interaction effect is presumed to exist in all cases in which different groups are introduced to a set of test items. It is the relative degree to which particular test items may vary between groups that is under is under test. Hence the hypothesis of interest is one of no difference in the interaction of Group 1 with item i compared to the interaction of Group 2 with the same item. This relationship may be expressed symbolically as follows:

$$H_0: \quad \Delta_{i1} - \Delta_{i2} = 0$$

against the alternative:

$$H_1: \quad \Delta_{i1} - \Delta_{i2} \neq 0$$

where Δ is an index of item difficulty. This is not, of course, really hypothesis testing in the formal sense of accepting or rejecting the null hypothesis by a statistical criterion, but it does offer a convenient model for conceptualizing the TID approach.

The Procedures

Procedurally, TID is rather straightforward. First, an index of item difficulty is generated for every item for each of two groups (e.g., p value). These indices are then converted, or transformed, to a standardized score, usually delta (Δ). The pair of normal deviates is plotted in a bivariate graph in which the Δ values for one group are plotted on the abscissa and those for the other are set along the ordinate. Next, a major axis line (that is, the straight line through which or closest to which most of the item plots fall) is fit to the data. Finally, a distance function, showing the minimum distance of each item from the major axis line, is computed. Bias is inferred for those items that are relatively distant from the line. Let us see how this procedure works in practice.

Figure 3 presents item plots representing actual data from the vocabulary subtest of an achievement battery administered to 58 Black and 168 White high school students (Cleary and Hilton, 1968). If the items were about equal in difficulty for both groups, the item plots would have fallen on or very near the 45-degree broken diagonal line. (This is the same point with TIDs that we saw earlier in the analysis of variance discussion in Figure 1. Remember, the two strategies are conceptually alike.) As can be seen in Figure 3, however, the item plots cluster below the diagonal. The major axis line, represented by the solid line, demonstrates that the items generally are more difficult for Black students. Item bias in this study was indicated by the divergence of each particular item plot from the lower major axis line. For example,

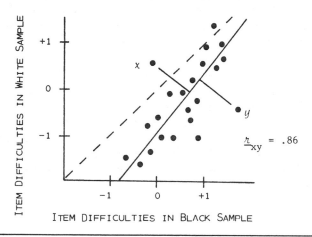

Figure 3: Bivariate Distribution of Item Difficulties; r_{xy} = .86
SOURCE: Pine (1977). Reprinted by permission.

the item labeled x plotted at a difficulty value of 0 for the Black students and approximately +0.5 for Whites. Thus this item was easier for Blacks than for Whites. The reverse is the case for the item labeled y. This item is easier for the the White students, exhibiting difficulty values of about −0.5 for Whites and +1.75 for Blacks. The correlation for all items between the two groups is .86, a moderate degree of linear relationship for the test as a whole.

Three statistical points are clearly displayed by the visual presentation of the data in Figure 3. These three points are: (1) 45 degrees is not an appropriate major axis line for these data; (2) the distance of each point to the correct *major axis line* (i.e., the line that minimizes perpendicular distances) must be measured; and most important, (3) the groups × items interaction contributes to the less than perfect correlation. The first two points call for mathematical calculations; the third is a conceptual realization. Let us examine this third point first.

By now it should be clear that the degree of heterogenity between groups on the attribute measured is directly proportional to the extent to which the pattern of plotted Δs deviate from r_{xy} = 1.00, a perfect correlation. The more difficult it is for one group to achieve a correct response on an item compared to another group, the further apart will be the pair of item plots; and also, the plotted points will depart from the major axis line by an ever greater distance. Bias is inferred for each item by the extent to which it may deviate from the major axis line. Recall with TIDs items are judged more or less biased by their relation to each other. The dispersion of the plotted items in Figure 2 displays this relational aspect of test item bias with TID methodology.

The first and second observations noted from Figure 3 are the calculations for determining the appropriate major axis line for the scatterplot of item difficulty values and computing the perpendicular distance of each item value from this line. These are the essential mathematics of the TID strategy to detect test item bias. Each of these calculations will be presented and described in a moment after discussion of procedures for transforming p values.

Transforming the Scale

The initial item difficulty indices are usually p values. Transforming p values themselves to other indices on a scale of at least interval level of measurement is a necessary step in the procedure. Albeit p values represent directly the proportional percentage of examinees passing a considered item, they do not represent item difficulty on an interval scale. The relationship between test item scores for two different groups must be linearly expressed in order to represent the item difficulty indices for both groups on a single scale with a common mean and standard deviation. In this way fair comparisons among item difficulties are possible.

Transformations of the p values to a normal deviate (i.e., standardized score) in TID methodology is typically to Δ. The Δ scale, which is equidistant for all points along the scale and allows for linear transformations, represents interval level of measurement with a mean of 13 and a standard deviation of 4. Simply, for item i of group j:

$$\Delta_{ij} = 4z_{ij} + 13 \qquad [3]$$

where z is the normal deviate with a mean of 0 and 1 for the standard deviation.

Deltas are used rather than the more often cited standard score z because Δs possess certain advantages over z values. They completely obviate negative values and are usually rounded to a single decimal. They can range from 0 to 26 corresponding to p values of .999 and .001, respectively. Higher Δ values represent more difficult items and lower Δs indicate easier items.

In addition to the features for Δ mentioned above, the standard error for Δ is constant at all levels of item difficulty. The standard error of a single proportion should be about .01 or less; if it is greater than that suspicion may be raised that the scattering of points may be attributed to sampling fluctuations. Erroneous conclusions regarding biased items may be the result for high rates of standard error. The standard error of Δ_{ij} is calculated:

$$SE_{\Delta_{ij}} = \frac{4}{N_j - 1} \qquad [4]$$

Deltas are nearly always used for the transformation of p values in TID methodology, but any transformation where z is $(1 - p)^{th}$ percentile of the standardized normal distribution will suffice (Merz, 1978).

Major Axis and Distance Points

In TID the degree of dispersion of the Δ plots on a bivariate graph is considered a measure of the groups $\times$ items interaction. This may be thought of as a sort of inverse of the correlation coefficient. A straight line, representing the major axis of the ellipse, may be drawn through a given scatterplot. This line serves as an index of the bivariate relationship of the Δ values for two groups. In biased item detection work it becomes the base standard from which judgments about particular aberrant items may be made. The major axis minimizes the distance between any set of Δ plots. This is not a true regression line although it is conceptually similar. This is so because the actual computations do not use exactly the same mathematics as a least squares regression solution does (see Shepard et al., 1980). One reason why regression formulae are not appropriate is that no valid rationale exists for deciding which group's deviation scores should be regressed onto the other. Regardless, the point remains that a major axis line that displays the minimum perpendicular distance of a given item is fit to the data.

Recall in regression theory that the *slope* of the major axis line indicates the change in Y with a change of one value of X. and the *intercept* is the point at which the regression line (or, in TID, the major axis of the elipse) touches the vertical axis. This relation is represented by

$$y = bx + a \qquad [5]$$

where b specifies the slope and a the intercept constant. Both the slope and the intercept must be calculated to mathematically define the line. The formulas for these calculations are given by Angoff and Ford (1973) as:

$$b = \frac{(\sigma_y^2 - \sigma_x^2) \pm \sqrt{(\sigma_y^2 - \sigma_x^2)^2 + 4r_{xy}^2 \sigma_x^2 \sigma_y^2}}{2r_{xy}\sigma_x\sigma_y} \qquad [6]$$

and

$$a = M_x - bM_y \qquad [7]$$

Recall that x and y are denotations for each of two groups considered, and σ_x and σ_y are the standard deviations for x and y, respectively. Also, M_x and M_y are the means for x and y, respectively; and finally, r_{xy} is the correlation coefficient between the groups' Δ values.

These calculations are rather straightforward. First, obtain the transformed item difficulties of each test item for both groups independently, and then compute the groups' means and standard deviations. Next, calculate the coefficient of correlation between the pair of Δs for each item. These values may now be rather conveniently applied to the formulas in equations 6 and 7. When the slope and intercept have been derived, the line may be entered onto the graph of plotted Δ pairs.

Now the distance function should be calculated. Remember, in TID main effects are not central to the detection of biased items; rather, interaction effects are studied. The perpendicular distance of any particular item plot from the major axis line is considered a function of the interaction of groups $\times$ items. The distance is given as:

$$D_i = \frac{bX_i + a - Y_i}{\sqrt{b^2 + 1}} \qquad [8]$$

where the b and a values are the slope and intercept point that were calculated by formulas 6 and 7. The X_i and Y_i values are the Δ scores for each group on a considered item i.

How Far Is Far?

When judging item bias as a distance function it is essential to determine at what point an item is lying beyond acceptable tolerance limits for displaying inherent bias. The question is fundamentally, "How far is far?" Various methods have been used to assess the limits for acceptable deviation. One of the more common approaches is to place confidence intervals about the major axis line. Item plots beyond these confidence limits may be judged aberrant. Bias is the conclusion for all outliers by this relative standard. The limit of $\pm.75$ z-score units away from the fixed line is often used for establishing acceptable boundaries of bias magnitude. For some purposes this standard is too rigorous for the realities of the inexact craft of skill or trait measurement, and the outlier limit may be fixed at ± 1.5 z-score units (see Merz and Grossen, 1979; Rudner, 1977).

Difficulties with TID

The biased item detection strategies associated with TIDs are grounded in the assumption that the interaction of groups $\times$ items is in fact a valid specification for identifying individual items aberrant from all others, and the degree of aberration may be considered a measure of test item bias. The rationale for this assumption was described above. Under certain circumstances, however, the assumption is not universally upheld. Hunter (1975), for example, demonstrated that if the items in a test are of varying difficulty (the usual case), groups $\times$ items interaction can exist in a perfectly unbiased test. Therefore, Hunter maintains, the definition of item bias as a significant groups $\times$ items interaction is inappropriate, and he suggests that some other criterion for bias be established.

Another significant limitation of TID methodology is that the proportion of correct answers is not a true measure of item difficulty, even when transformed from p values to a Δ by the inverse normal transformation. This is so because two different groups cannot usually be expected to perform equally well on a test, and when this is the case, the plotted points do not fall on a straight line at all; instead, they form a curve. Now, if two different levels of discriminating power exist for the items (one for each group), the plotted Δs could actually fall on two different curves. Unequal comparisons can be the result. The rationale for this argument involves mathematical examination of item characteristic curves and is complex beyond our present scope (see Lord, 1980).

There is yet another shortcoming with TID methodology. The proportion of students correctly responding to an item as indicated by Δ in TIDs describes not only the test item but also the group tested. While some circumstances make this characteristic defensible, it also greatly inhibits any generalizability of findings beyond the specific sample tested. In many more settings external validity is of critical importance, and this lack is a severe limitation. These final two limitations of TID methodology are also true of the ANOVA strategy discussed in Chapter 2.

Variations of TID

Variations of TID bias detection tactics as explicated above—the traditional explanation—abound. Many strike at specific flaws with the technique, while others aim at extending the approach. A few variations, those most practical, will be described. Rudner, Getson, and Knight (1980a, 1980b) and Merz and Grossen (1979) describe a modification of the original TID procedure. This alternative uses group item means and standard deviations to transform p values to within-group standard scores, z. When using this method in a study with simulated data, the distance function from a 45-degree major axis line was computed by the method just described; however, the slope of the line was arbitrarily defined as one (i.e., b = 1). Conceptually, this modification remains very close to the traditional TID strategy, but there is no attempt to straighten the line of relationship—called "linearize"—between the two groups. The attempt here is to avoid the theoretical objections to the inverse normal transformation. The approach is sensitive to item difficulty but insensitive to bias in item discrimination.

Echternacht's (1974) modification to the TID approach, like Rudner's, assumes a fixed item-line of 45 degrees. After calculating Δs for each group in the usual manner, Echternacht tests the distribution in the differences for Δ for normality rather than comparing Δs against each other. This tests the distribution $\Delta_{i1} - \Delta_{i2}$ for normality with the mean and variance of the differences as parameters. The parameters are considered as confidence bounds about which inferences for identifying biased and unbiased items may be drawn. This procedure is essentially a goodness-of-fit test of the Kolmogorov-Smirnov type. Under this test the differences are distributed normally, but the mean and variance are unknown.

Another alternative TID approach is offered by Jensen (1980). In this approach the groups $\times$ items interaction for identification of biased items is exploited in a slightly different manner. The interaction of group $\times$ items is composed of two elements: disordinal effects (the result of items having differing rank orders of difficulties between two groups) and ordinal effects (the consequence of relative differences in item difficulties regardless of identical rank orders for both groups). Disordinal effects alone can be considered a powerful indication of biased items between groups. The disordinal effects may be observed by calculating the rank order correlation (Spearman's rho, ρ) and considering $1 - \rho^2$ an estimate of the purely disordinal aspect of the groups $\times$ items interaction. The Pearson correlation coefficient (r) may be employed to estimate the ordinal effects, thus allowing for comparison of the disordinal with the ordinal effects. Here, the r is not calculated on the values themselves; instead, the proposal is to use a modified statistic, called Δ decrements. The decrements are computed by calculating the distance between ranked (highest to lowest) Δs (e.g., $\Delta_1 - \Delta_2, \Delta_2 - \Delta_3, \ldots$). Delta decrements are obtained within each group, and r is computed on the Δ decrements for each group. The value $\rho^2(1 - r^2)$ is considered an estimate of the purely ordinal effects of the groups $\times$ items interaction. The residual portion (i.e., the joint contribution to the interaction variance of both ordinal and disordinal effects) of the groups $\times$ items interaction is $\rho^2 r^2$.

A slightly different tack is presently being explored by Sticker (1981), and at least in this early developmental stage, appears to offer some real advantages over the traditional TID approach while retaining its basic features and benefits. A correlation, labeled a partial correlation index, between success on a considered item and group membership with true score, or an examinee's expected score, partialed out is computed. This approach includes the much-desired criterion method in which ability is controlled. The partial correlation index theoretically overcomes a principal limitation of the TID approach (namely, its inability to define item difficulties independently of the sample groups) while retaining its comparative simplicity. Stricker (1982) is investing the application of this modified TID in empirical settings.

From this brief review it can be seen that a variety of approaches exist under the common umbrella of TID methodology. To use any particular single approach is advisable only when one realizes the strengths and limitations of the various alternatives. The next two bias detection strategies discussed (chi square and item characteristic curve) approach the problem of bias item identification with a wholly new point of view and with very different assumptions. Let us go forward to explore these new approaches.

4. CHI SQUARE

The chi-square (χ^2) approach to the identification of test item bias examines the likelihood—or probability—of test takers from different groups with the same ability levels correctly responding to an item. An item is considered unbiased when all persons at a given ability level have an equal probability of correctly answering an item regardless of their group membership as to ethnicity, sex, age, or other discrete subpopulation. The essential strategy of this technique is to remove biased item identification from the dependency on the groups $\times$ items interaction as the arbiter of bias. Recall that analysis of variance and transformed item difficulty approaches rely almost exclusively on the assumption that groups $\times$ items interaction is a valid indicator of bias within items. To overcome the difficulties that may exist in this assumption, chi square approaches to identifying biased items are oriented in a different direction. Instead, with χ^2 strategy, the proportion of responses within ability categories for two groups diverse in some given criterion is examined.

The technique is of the goodness-of-fit type in that from the null hypothesis of no difference a significance test is made between an expected number of examinee responses in a particular ability level category and the actual number that was observed to respond in that category. Thus the χ^2 approach to test item bias is sensitive to within-groups item discrimination in addition to giving attention to differences among groups in item difficulty levels.

Procedurally, the total test score is divided into a specified number of categories, each of which represents a particular ability stratum. The ability levels are considered independently of one another and irrespective of their rank order. A variety of hypotheses, each serving a slightly different purpose, may then be tested. But the principal intention is to examine the degree of difference between score interval proportions for the two groups as they actually distributed themselves compared with what may be the expected frequencies of response. We will look into several of these alternative hypotheses and present the procedural steps required for their introduction and use.

The χ^2 approach to investigating bias in test items represents a significant departure from the ANOVA and TID strategies. In addition to abandoning the presumption of bias as a significant groups $\times$ items interaction, the χ^2 technique uses a wholly different graphic presentation for displaying item characteristics. Rather than plotting item difficulty indices for all items from each of two groups on a bivariate graph as was done in ANOVA and TID, the χ^2 strategy plots each item individually in item characteristic curves (ICC). For any given test item, the ICC represents the relationship between the chances of a correct response on the item and examinees' total ability in the trait being measured by the set of items contained in the test. ICCs are one very useful way of organizing performance data about a test item when administered to a variety of heterogeneous subjects.

In test theory an item is presumed to be perfectly matched (in terms of difficulty) to an individual when the examinee has a fifty-fifty chance of getting the item correct (Warm, 1978). If the examinee has odds of a correct response on the item less than .5, the item may be too difficult to assess the trait with validity; conversely, greater than .5 odds and the item may be too easy for accurate trait measurement. In test theory "odds" are technically termed *probability of a correct response.* Item characteristic curves display the probability of a correct response for an examinee at varying ability levels.

A hypothetical ICC is presented in Figure 4. Notice in Figure 4 that the ability variable is continuous, and the probability of success on the item is considered a function of any given ability level. Total ability for a particular examinee is estimated by that person's score on the entire test. A major assumption of the χ^2 approach to test item bias is that total test scores yield a valid indicator of ability. If the test is multichotomized into subtests, ability is measured only by the subgroup of items containing the particular item under consideration. Also notice in the ICC in Figure 4 that ICCs are not straight lines that linearize the relationship between probability for success and examinee ability; rather, they are usually S-shaped curves that begin very low and rise monotonically with increases in examinee ability.

Comparing ICCs between groups is a very useful exercise in test bias investigations. Specifically, items are said to be unbiased if item

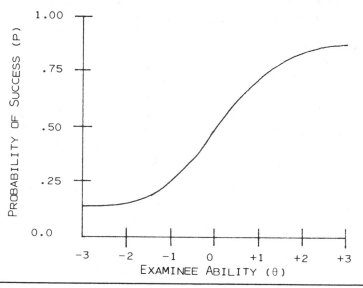

Figure 4: A Hypothetical Item Characteristic Curve

test scores for two groups generate identical ICCs. That is, two groups have an equal probability of answering an item correctly such that item discrimination (slope) is the same, item difficulty (inflection point) is the same, and a correct response for guessing when ability is very low is equally probable (lower asymptote).

There are several mathematical functions that could serve to describe the form of an ICC, and we shall explore one of them that is particularly useful for identifying bias in test items when we consider the item characteristic curve of the logistic response model in Chapter 5. There we shall deal with ICCs in a slightly more technically sophisticated manner; for now, however, it is sufficient simply to conceptualize the ICC as descriptive of individual test items. Readers wishing to further explore ICCs as well as the related test information curve (TIC) and item information functions (ITF) are referred to Baker (1977), Hambleton (1979), and Lord (1980).

One difference between χ^2 and item characteristic curve approaches, however, is that in the χ^2 approach the ability dimension is divided into discrete categories, usually four or five, and within each category the probability of a correct response is assumed to be constant. The resultant item characteristic curve rises in rectangular steps, each of which is approximately the height of the curve within any given ability range. This is slightly different from the smooth upward curve denoting increasing ability of the three-parameter latent trait model item characteristic curve. For this ICC model it is necessary to estimate mathematically each of the item parameters. The χ^2 item characteristic curve avoids these technically difficult steps. Although graphing the item curves is theoretically possible in the χ^2 technique, it is not done in practice. Instead, a goodness-or-fit test is applied procedurally to tabulated scores.

In addition to the positive value of possessing a common logic with latent trait models, there are other advantages to using the χ^2 for biased item detection. The chi-square statistic is comparatively simple to compute, usable by researchers with little statistical background, and readily comprehended by laypersons. Also, the technique does not require the very large sample sizes that are a prerequisite to the latent trait models and often difficult to obtain, particularly for certain ethnic minority populations. Thus the χ^2 bias item detection technique is frequently used in practical settings and probably follows only the transformed item difficulties approach in popularity among methods to investigate item bias.

A variety of techniques exist for identifying biased items that employ the chi-square statistic or a statistic similar to chi square. I will explore several of these as well as describe situations in which each may be appropriate. But first some commonalities for all χ^2 item bias procedures.

Establishing Ability Levels

Establishing the ability levels on the total score scale is a first step in any of the χ^2 procedures. Ability levels are merely score intervals where the total score is partitioned into a number of discrete categories. This step must be done with care and full recognition that expected frequencies in the chi-square statistic, and hence significance testing, can be artifically altered by manipulation of the score intervals chosen. The terms *score interval* and *ability level* will be used interchangeably since it is assumed in the technique that total scores do accurately represent ability of examinees. The problems of fair choice in establishing ability intervals may be exacerbated when the cell frequencies are very small. About ten to twenty observed correct responses per cell is a recommended minimum in any case. Typically, this will result in about three to five ability categories. For large sample sizes, increase the number of ability score intervals or the minimum cell frequencies required. A partial score distribution with ability levels established is presented in Table 2. The data displayed in the table are actual scores for one item from a study of test item bias conducted during item analysis of the *Metropolitan Readiness Test* (Scheuneman, 1979). Table 2 will be used throughout the discussion of χ^2 procedures to illustrate various alternative techniques.

Note in Table 2 that the subtest in the example contains 14 items. The total number of examinees was 797, and they were distributed by four score intervals: 1 to 9, 10 and 11, 12, and 13 and 14. The four score intervals were established using correct scores only; incorrect responses were not taken into account in the present example, although we will consider them in subsequent examples of χ^2 strategies.

Choosing ability intervals by simply dividing the sample population into some number of categories, say quartiles or quintiles, appears obvious but is not recommended. Often the highest and lowest ability intervals will be underrepresented due to a typically wide disparity in sizes of the groups as well as the relative difficulty of the item between groups. Intervals should be selected so that the smallest cell frequency is approximately equal for each ability interval. It is important that wrong choices also be considered in selecting ability intervals. When no attention is paid to frequency of incorrect responses, the high extreme categories can become compressed often with just one or two score points comprising the entire ability interval. An item statistic may become distorted when it does not discriminate within either group but greatly discriminates between (or among) groups. Such is the case of an item easily gotten correct by most of the examinees in one group and missed by most of those in another group. Finally, ability levels are not fixed throughout the investigation for all the considered items in a test. The intervals must be determined individually for each item. When items do possess identical scores or ability intervals it is coincidental. The operation of establishing ability intervals for items may appear rather straightforward, but be cautioned: It can be a frustrating exercise.

Notation

A brief description of the notation used to represent the bias models may be in order here since we shall rely on it heavily for this discussion

TABLE 2

Partial Frequency Data for Two Groups on One Test Item

Score Interval	Number of Examinees			Obtained Frequencies			Proportion Correct	Expected Frequencies	
	Group 1	Group 2	Total	Group 1	Group 2	Total		Group 1	Group 2
13-14	25	315	340	22	300	322	.95	23.68	298.32
12	24	110	134	18	99	117	.87	20.96	96.04
10-11	48	118	166	23	93	116	.70	33.54	82.46
1-9	65	92	157	14	33	47	.30	19.46	27.54
Total	162	635	797	77	525	602			

SOURCE: Scheuneman, Janice. "A Method of Assessing Bias in Test Items." *Journal of Educational Measurement*, Fall 1979. Copyright 1979, National Council on Measurement in Education, Washington, D.C. Reprinted by permission.

of chi-square approaches. The mathematical model will describe several groups although only two groups are considered in the examples to follow. The model is: F_{ijk} equals (=) the frequency of occurrence in the ith group measured in the jth score interval of the test for response level k. And, that in the general situation:

$$i = 1, 2, \ldots, I$$

$$j = 1, 2, \ldots, J$$

and

k = 1, if the response is a success.

k = 2, if the response is a failure.

Also, P_{ij1} is the probability of success for subjects in the ith group measured in the jth score interval. Finally, the probability of an incorrect response (i.e., failure) may be expressed as:

$$P_{ij2} = 1 - P_{ij1} \hspace{4cm} [9]$$

The Methods

There are a variety of statistical methods available for investigating test item bias based upon χ^2 procedures. Several of them will be described, but it should be noted that they may not be thought of as indiscriminate nor can they be used interchangeably. Each statistic tests a separate hypothesis, and the determination of which hypothesis is under consideration will in great part dictate the appropriate choice of methods.

Marascuilo and Slaughter (1981a, 1981b) suggest six procedures for detecting biased items. All of them are based on chi-square statistics, and they are the preferred χ^2 methods. Not all are presented here because some deal with specialized circumstances and others require statistical procedures advanced beyond the level dealt with in this introductory monograph; however, two methods, those most practical, will be described. For the others the interested reader well versed in statistics is referred to the primary source.

Marascuilo Method One. Marascuilo Method One is a series of pairwise comparisons of conditional probabilities in 2×2 contingency tables. The test, the Fisher Exact Test of Equal Proportions, is used to interrogate the differences in p values between groups at each ability level. For item bias investigations, Method One may be expressed symbolically as follows:

$$\Delta_j = P_{1j1} - P_{2j1} = 0 \qquad [10]$$

such that Δ_j (the Δ at any given ability level) equals the difference between the probability of a correct response for Group 1 at the score (i.e., ability level) interval j and the probability of a correct response for Group 2 (at the same score interval); and this difference equals zero. Bias is concluded for an item any time this difference does not equal zero ($\Delta_j \neq 0$) at any particular score interval. If an item is unbiased the probability of responding correctly to the item is equal for all groups considered and at each level of ability. Symbolically this may be expressed:

$$P_{1j1} = P_{2j1} = \ldots = P_{ij1} = P_{j1} \qquad [11]$$

That is, the probability of successfully answering an item for examinees in Group 1 at score level j is equal to the probability of successfully answering an item for examinees in Group 2 at the same score interval, and so on for as many discrete groups as are considered. This is a symbolic representation of the definition of item bias under chi-square procedures: Simply, when all persons regardless of subgroup membership, at any given ability level have an equal chance of success on an item, the item is considered unbiased.

With Marascuilo Method One for two groups the hypotheses and alternatives under test are simply the set of j pairwise comparisons:

$$H_{0(1)}: \Delta_1 = P_{111} - P_{211} = 0 \qquad H_{1(1)}: \Delta_1 \neq 0$$

$$H_{0(2)}: \Delta_2 = P_{121} - P_{221} = 0 \qquad H_{1(2)}: \Delta_2 \neq 0$$

$$\vdots \qquad\qquad\qquad \vdots$$

$$H_{0(j)}: \Delta_j = P_{1j1} - P_{2j1} = 0 \qquad H_{1(j)}: \Delta_j \neq 0$$

These may be read as follows: Null hypothesis for score interval 1: Delta (already described) at score interval 1 equals the difference between probability of Group 1, at score interval 1, for a correct response (1) and the probability of Group 2, at score interval 1, for a correct response (1); and this difference equals zero. The alternative hypothesis is that the difference does not equal zero. These pairwise statements are the comparisons at each of the ability levels.

Using this model the data presented in Table 2 may be rewritten as a series of 2×2 contingency tables, one for each ability level. Table 3 presents the contingency tables. It is also important to note that the data in the table have been expanded to include the incorrect response rates for each group as well as the correct responses.

In order to test the hypotheses it is necessary to obtain values for the probability of success on an item. This must be done at each ability level and independently for all items considered. We learned from equation 11 that for any item to be considered unbiased the probability of a correct response must be equal for all groups within the same ability level. Therefore, the unbiased estimate of P_{ij1} at any ability level across both groups is the cumulative correct response rate, or frequency of occurrence, for all groups within the considered score interval divided by the total number of subjects in all groups at the same score interval. Or, symbolically:

$$P_{.j1} = \frac{F_{1j1} + F_{2j1} + \ldots + F_{ij1}}{N_{1j.} + N_{2j.} + \ldots + N_{ij.}} \qquad [12]$$

where: F_{1j1} is the frequency of occurrence in the first group measured in the jth score interval for a correct (e.g., 1) response.

and: N_{ij} is the number of subjects in the ith group for score interval j.

Applying equation 12 to the data in Table 3, the unbiased estimates of the unknown parameters calculate as:

$$P_{.11} = \frac{14 + 33}{65 + 92} = \frac{47}{157} = 0.2994 \qquad P_{.12} = \frac{51 + 59}{65 + 92} = \frac{110}{157} = 0.7006$$

$$P_{.12} = \frac{23 + 93}{48 + 118} = \frac{116}{166} = 0.6988 \qquad P_{.22} = \frac{25 + 25}{48 + 118} = \frac{50}{166} = 0.3012$$

$$P_{.31} = \frac{18 + 99}{24 + 110} = \frac{117}{134} = 0.8731 \qquad P_{.32} = \frac{6 + 11}{24 + 110} = \frac{17}{134} = 0.1269$$

$$P_{.41} = \frac{22 + 300}{25 + 315} = \frac{300}{340} = 0.9471 \qquad P_{.42} = \frac{3 + 15}{25 + 315} = \frac{18}{340} = 0.0529$$

For chi-square procedures the expected frequencies must also be obtained. Expressed in terms of the estimate of P_{ij1}, the expected frequencies may be derived by the following symbolic formula:

$$F_{ij1} = N_{ij.} P_{ij1} \qquad\qquad [13]$$

For the data in Table 3 at score interval 1-9 for Group 1 these values are:

$$F_{111} = N_{11.} P_{.11} = 65 (0.2994) = 19.46$$

and

$$F_{112} = N_{11.} P_{.12} = 65 (0.7006) = 45.54$$

The remaining expected values are reported in the upper right-hand corner of each cell in Table 3.

Each of the hypotheses outlined by Marascuilo Method One procedures is now ready for testing by the test of equality of two proportions using the hypergeometric distribution. Or, more simply stated, it is a case of two independent samples and the test is to determine whether two groups differ in the proportion with which they fall into one or the other of two mutually exclusive categories.

Fisher's Exact Test. For small samples the appropriate statistic is the Fisher's exact probability test. For this test the data must be represented as frequencies (i.e., number of subjects) in a 2 × 2 contingency table. This test yields a ratio of the exact probability of the observed occurrence and is computed by taking the product of the factorials of the four marginal totals divided by the product of N factorial multiplied by the cell frequencies factorial.

When the sample sizes are large, as in the present example in Table 3, with 162 subjects in Group 1 and 635 subjects in Group 2, the Fisher's exact probability test is not appropriate; the calculations become

TABLE 3
Contingency Tables for Two Groups at Four
Total Score Intervals on One Test Item

SCORE INTERVAL 1-9	GROUP 1	GROUP 2
+	19.46 / 14	27.54 / 33
0	45.54 / 51	64.46 / 59

$$\chi_1^2 = 3.75$$

SCORE INTERVAL 12	GROUP 1	GROUP 2
+	20.95 / 18	96.04 / 99
0	3.05 / 6	13.96 / 11

$$\chi_3^2 = 3.99$$

SCORE INTERVAL 10-11	GROUP 1	GROUP 2
+	33.54 / 23	82.46 / 93
0	14.46 / 25	35.54 / 25

$$\chi_2^2 = 15.47 \ (p < .01)$$

SCORE INTERVAL 13-14	GROUP 1	GROUP 2
+	23.68 / 22	298.34 / 300
0	1.32 / 3	16.66 / 15

$$\chi_4^2 = 2.42$$

+ = success on item.
0 = failure on item.

tedious and the numbers so large that they are out of range for many calculators. It is recommended for large numbers of cases that the tests be approximated by the familiar normal curve statistics on variables with chi-square distribution. The degrees of freedom is set at one (i.e., $\gamma = 1$) in such circumstances.

Finally, for significance testing an arbitrary level for probability must be set, but the decision need not be made with out guidelines. The decision rule for Type I (α) error can be controlled by partitioning the total risk of α across the number of tests to be performed. This may be represented as:

$$\alpha = \frac{1}{j} \alpha_t$$

For example, in the case of the item from the *Metropolitan Readiness Test* (data in Tables 2 and 3) there are four ability level categories (j = 4). If α = .05, each test for the equality of two proportions should be performed with one quarter of the risk associated with it. That is

$$\alpha = \frac{1}{4}(0.05) = 0.0125$$

In the example the critical value of χ^2 at .0125 is 6.25. When $\chi_j^2 > 6.25$ bias may be concluded. For the data presented in Table 3, the χ^2 value at each score interval is: $\chi_1^2 = 3.75$, $\chi_2^2 = 15.47$, $\chi_3^2 = 3.99$, and $\chi_4^2 = 2.42$. Since χ_2^2 exceeds the critical value, item bias is seen to exist in this considered item for the second ability level of examinees.

Marascuilo Method Three. Marascuilo Method Three is an alternative to Marascuilo Method One when it is believed that item bias against one specific group may be present at all ability levels, and not just that bias may exist at some ability level. The assumption of Marascuilo Method Three is that if a difference exists, it is constant for all ability levels. Method One describes the P_{ij1} for every ability level and does not make this assumption. Thus Method Three is a more powerful test and is recommended over Method One whenever differences are constant across all ability levels.

Symbolically the hypothesis under test by Marascuilo Method Three is:

$$H_0: \Delta_1 = \Delta_2 = \ldots = \Delta_j = 0$$

against:

$$H_1: \Delta_1 = \Delta_2 = \ldots = \Delta_j = \Delta_0$$

where Δ_0 is a common value, and assume $\Delta_0 < 0$.

The hypothesis for Method Three states that there are no differences in a Δ (i.e., probability differences between groups) at ability 1, 2, . . . j. In other words, the Δs at each ability level (e.g., $P_{1j1} - P_{2j2}$) equal zero. The alternative hypothesis states that differences in groups at every ability level are the same (Δ_0).

In the latent trait theory terms, the test of hypotheses by Marascuilo Method Three is one of parallelism of the operating item characteristic curves. If the null hypothesis is rejected, it may be concluded that different difficulty levels exist for the items, and the lower asymptote of the item characteristic curves were different for the two groups. Bias is inferred to be present.

Irwin-Fisher Tests. There are at least four procedures available to test these hypotheses (Marascuilo and McSweeney, 1977). These tests are generally referred to as combined Irwin-Fisher tests. Two of these tests, one by Maxwell and the other by Cochran, will be described.

Maxwell's statistic for the parallelism test is:

$$Z_M = \frac{1}{\sqrt{J}} \sum_{j=1}^{J} Z_j \qquad\qquad [14]$$

The value Z_M relates to the standard normal distribution. The critical value for hypothesis testing associated with a particular significance level may be read from a table of probabilities for the normal distribution.

Again referring to the data in Table 3, the calculations for equation 14 are:

$$Z_M = \frac{1}{\sqrt{4}} (-1.94 - 3.93 - 2.00 - 1.56) = -4.71$$

For $\alpha = 0.05$, the level of $Z_{0.05} = -1.645$. Thus the hypothesis of no difference in Δ at all levels is rejected; Δ_0 is presumed to exist.

There is a second procedure, developed by Cochran, to test this same hypothesis. In Cochran's approach confidence intervals are established for Δ_0. Item characteristic curves may be checked for uniformity of displacement at all levels of ability. Figure 5 illustrates the concept. The point to note from the figure is the displacement between the two lines at each of the four score categories. The displacement appears similar for the mid-values of each of the four ability level categories, indicating that Method Three may be preferred in this example over Method One. By this method, one relates:

$$Z_C = \frac{\hat{\Delta}_0}{SE_{\hat{\Delta}_0}} \qquad [15]$$

to the standard normal distribution. By the theory of least squares the following equations are given for estimating Δ_0 and the standard error of $\hat{\Delta}_0$:

$$\hat{\Delta}_0 = \frac{\sum\limits_{j=1}^{J} W_j \hat{\Delta}_j}{\sum\limits_{j=1}^{J} W_j} \qquad [16]$$

and

$$SE_{\hat{\Delta}_0}^2 = \frac{1}{\left(\sum\limits_{j=1}^{J} W_j\right)^2} \sum\limits_{j=1}^{J} W_j P_{.j1} p_{.j2}$$

where

$$W_j = \frac{N_{1j.} N_{2j.}}{N_{1j.} + N_{2j.}} \qquad [17]$$

Although formidable looking, these formulae may be conveniently worked through. Once again, relating these equations to the data presented in the exampled item in Table 3:

$$\hat{\Delta}_1 = \frac{14}{65} - \frac{33}{92} = -0.1433 \qquad W_1 = 38.0892$$

$$\hat{\Delta}_2 = \frac{23}{48} - \frac{93}{113} = -0.3089 \qquad W_2 = 34.1205$$

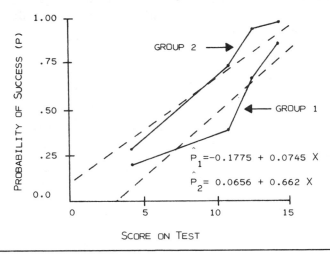

Figure 5: Best-Fitting Straight Lines

SOURCE: Marascuilo and Slaughter (1981b). Reprinted by permission.

$$\hat{\Delta}_3 = \frac{18}{24} - \frac{99}{110} = -0.1500 \qquad W_3 = 19.7015$$

$$\hat{\Delta}_4 = \frac{22}{25} - \frac{300}{315} = -0.0724 \qquad W_4 = 23.1618$$

so that

$$\hat{\Delta}_0 = -0.1793 \qquad SE_{\hat{\Delta}_0} = 0.0374$$

and

$$Z_C = \frac{-0.1793}{0.0374} = -4.79$$

Again, $\alpha = 0.05$ and $Z_{0.05} = 1.645$, and as before the value $Z_C = -4.79$ rejects the hypotheses of identical operating item characteristic curves.

A further feature of note is available to investigators using Cochran's approach. It is the final step, establishing the confidence interval itself. Here:

$$\Delta_0 < \hat{\Delta}_o + Z_{1-\alpha} SE_{\hat{\Delta}_0}$$

$$< -.1793 + 1.645 \, (0.0374)$$

$$< -0.18 + 0.06$$

$$< -0.12 \qquad\qquad [18]$$

The conclusion drawn from the example data is that the probability of correctly answering the item for Group 1 examinees is at least 12 percentage points below that of Group 2 examinees at all levels of the test. Thus bias is seen to exist against Group 1 examinees at all ability levels. Note the difference of this conclusion of bias at all ability levels from that of Marascuilo Method One in which it was concluded that bias was present at only one ability level. This example points out the importance of understanding the hypothesis under scrutiny by any of the biased item detection strategies.

Summary. These two Marascuilo methods for detecting test item bias are based on χ^2 statistics and in many circumstances offer the preferred route for investigation. In general they are not difficult to compute and the findings are easier to explain to nontechnically trained individuals than are some of the other bias investigation strategies. Marascuilo Method One is the most simple and has the widest applicability to research problems; simply, equal proportions of respondents divided by a criterion variable are investigated by either the J Fisher exact test or, with large samples, the Pearson test of homogeneity with $\gamma = 1$. Marascuilo Method Three is preferred over Method One whenever one suspects a specific item to be biased against one of the two groups at all ability levels. Again, the context and purposes for investigating bias in test items will influence the choice of an appropriate methodology.

Prior to Marascuilo's work, the most often cited χ^2 methodology was one proposed by Scheuneman (1979). This is described as a modified χ^2 or a "statistic similar to χ^2." It has been noted by several investigators that the Scheuneman index will not distribute as the χ^2 model requires because only correct responses are considered (see Baker, 1981; Merz and Grosson, 1979; Rudner et al., 1980a). This technique has been superseded by the Marascuilo methods and is not now recommended.

The chi square is a useful approach to bias item investigation. The χ^2 statistic, while theoretically nonparametric, can prove a powerful indicator of test item bias when correctly used. The procedures outlined in this chapter will aid in finding the appropriate method when chi-square statistics are considered.

5. ITEM CHARACTERISTIC CURVE

Item Response Theory (IRT)

Latent trait theory is a viewpoint applicable to test development. Simply put, latent traits are examinee characteristics that cause a consistent performance on a test of any given cognitive skill or achievement or ability. A trait is not a hypothetical construct; rather, it may be thought of as an intervening variable between what is there and what can be measured. It causes a test performance. Latent trait theories have been developed and applied under several rubrics, but we shall use the one that most clearly emphasizes the psychologically based nature of latent traits theories, item reponse theory (IRT). It is from IRT that the item characteristic curve (ICC) approaches to the detection and correction of test item bias are derived. Certainly ICC approaches are the most elegant of all the models discussed to tease out test item bias. ICC techniques are also the most difficult to understand conceptually and are extremely complex procedurally. Computer processing of data is the only practical way the ICC methods may be exploited. Fortunately, much work is being done in the field and some of this is directed toward making latent trait theories more approachable by persons less well versed in statistics and test theory and methods.

The issues involved in item response theory are too large and encompassing to detail here, and several excellent descriptions are available. A technical introduction is given by Birnbaum (1968), developments in latent trait and related issues are discussed by Hambleton (1979), and a primer of item response theory is given by Warm (1978); also, an excellent discussion of the models of IRT is provided by Baker (1977). The following discussion assumes the reader is fundamentally familiar with at least some of the models of latent trait theory and therefore (more deliberately here than in any other section of this monograph) some relevant material is omitted. The presumed acquaintance of the reader will be on IRT generally; its applicability to test item bias will be the focus for the following discussion.

A definition for test item bias using IRT concepts has been proposed by Pine (1977):

> A test is unbiased if all individuals having the same underlying ability have an equal probability of getting the item correct, regardless of subgroup membership.

Recall the definition used for chi-square (χ^2) approaches to test item bias was similar to this ICC definition. Conceptually, the two approaches are alike. Actually, the fact that χ^2 strategies approximate ICC methods is one of its attractive features. However, χ^2 approaches, while much easier to work with procedurally, do not contain the power of ICC methods. Still, the notion for both is that item characteristic curves generated for each of two groups should be alike for an item to be considered unbiased. We shall explore the item curve itself in detail a little later on.

While the item characteristic curve is not actually computed in χ^2 procedures (and only theoretically noted), in ICC methodology it is in fact derived. It presents all the available information for analysis of bias between groups. Of particular interest in the ICC approach is the statistical independence of persons and items. The separate estimation of these parameters by the IRT model provides an avenue to biased item detection that avoids the difficulties in traditional or classical test theory yet still satisfies the criterion of a consistent definition of item bias.

The independence of persons from describing items and vice versa is a departure from classical test theory and methods. As was demonstrated earlier with the χ^2, TID, ANOVA, as well as other biased item detection techniques, severe problems for biased item work persist in procedures based on classical test models. Inherent in some of the assumptions of classical test theory is the notion that item characteristics are situation or sample specific. This means that p values (proportion of examinees correctly responding to an item), point-biserial correlations (an item discrimination indication between an item alternative and the test), examinees' aggregate score (means and standard deviations and standard error), skewness and kurtosis, and other indices are all dependent on the sample of examinees under study. Since the sample of examinees will of course change with each new administration of the test, the statistics will also change. Likewise, item discrimination is not invariant across groups of examinees who differ in ability. Finally, a further limitation of test item bias methods based on classical test models is that generalizability of results for either the test item to a new sample of examinees or a new item to the same examinee sample is dubious.

Because of these shortcomings much attention in the field of bias item detection is being directed toward ICC approaches. Let us begin our discussion of ICC strategies to detect test item bias with a look at the underlying assumptions.

Assumptions of IRT

The difference in assumptions used to develop the test theory and methods between classical test models and IRT are enormous and important. An internalized grasp of these differences is key to realizing the advantages IRT holds for test item bias methodology. There are three main assumptions for IRT. They are: (1) dimensionality of the latent space, (2) local independence of items, and (3) item characteristic curves. Each of these will be described. These assumptions mean that the test of item bias—the functions in the item characteristic curves—must display probabilities of a correct response for an item equally across different population groups of the same ability. In ICC methodology, the classification of an item as unbiased is dependent on the shape of the item characteristic curve.

The first assumption of IRT is dimensionality of the latent space. In this context dimensionality means that an examinee's performance on a test can be attributed to a single trait or ability. Traditionally the trait or ability or subject matter knowledge is referred to by theta (θ). Theoretically, one possesses an ability or trait in amounts ranging from not at all to complete mastery; the continuum is from minus infinity to plus infinity [$-\infty \leqslant \theta \leqslant +\infty$]. In practical work with IRT, however, θ rarely exceeds the range [$-3, +3$]. Also, the θ values of a sample need not necessarily be normally distributed.

Tests that consider a single trait are called *unidimensional*. Examples of unidimensional tests could be reading, language, and mathematical achievement tests; some ability tests, such as numerical, verbal, or spatial relationships tests; tests of mechanical comprehensions; and the like. The practicalities of score interpretation make the assumption of unidimensionality almost universally accepted by test constructors. Items from a unidimensional test may or may not correlate highly with each other, but only a single ability accounts for an examinee's correctly responding to an item or set of test items.

The second assumption of IRT is local independence for items. This assumption of local independence means an examinee's performance on any item is unaffected by the performance on any other item in the test. Item scores in such a circumstance are said to be statistically independent. If a test is truly unidimensional, as the first assumption for IRT states, the assumption of local independence for items is necessarily satisfied. Therefore, for any test in which these assumptions are met a single trait is measured N times independently, where N is the number of items. In the aggregate these N independent measurements make up a set of items as in a subtest or whole test.

Local independence also presumes the probability for an examinee that item scores will fall in any pattern is simply the product of occurrence of the scores on each item of the test. This may be demonstrated in the following manner. Assume the probability of the occurrence of a five-item response pattern is V. Also:

1 = correct response
0 = incorrect response

and:

P_i = the probability of a correct response
$1 - P_i$ = the probability of an incorrect response

Suppose the pattern of the occurrence of a five-item response is

$$V = (1, 0, 1, 1, 0)$$

Then:

$$V_T = P_1. (1 - P_2) .P_3.P_4. (1 - P_5) \tag{19}$$

Thus the total probability is the product of the independent item response rates. Note also that P_i is specific to a particular ability level. A statistical test to check the independence of item response for examinees is available (see Lord, 1952).

The third IRT assumption concerns the item characteristic curves and is the most descriptive assumption for identifying test item bias using the ICC approach. Although the item characteristic curves were briefly described and used in the earlier discussion of χ^2 approaches to investigate test item bias, in the ICC strategy they are utilized more fully and hence a more thorough and detailed explanation is required.

As before, the item characteristic curve is a graphic representation of a mathematical function that describes the probability of an examinee's correctly answering a test item relative to the ability measured by the total set of items in the test. This mathematical function is designated:

$$P_i(\theta)$$

where:

   P = probability of a correct response
   i = any given item
   θ = the ability under scrutiny by the test

The item characteristic curve displays this function. A hypothetical item characteristic curve was presented in Figure 4. The IRT model that has most applicability to test item bias methodology is the logistic response model and is represented by the smooth S-shaped curve of the item characteristic curve. This curve is the regression of item scores on ability. For any given ability level the curve will remain the same for every subgroup of examinees. Theoretical statisticians have been able to verify this by demonstrating that when the complete latent space is defined for all examinees, and ICC will remain invariant across populations of examinees (see Lord, 1980). The *probability* that an examinee will respond correctly to an item depends upon the shape of the curve (i.e., ICC form) alone.

The probability of a correct response is independent of the examinee ability in the group considered. This is not to imply that P is independent of θ—in fact, as described, P is a function of θ—but merely that the concept that a given examinee's probability of getting an item correct depends on the examinee's overall ability in the construct being measured rather than on the degree of difficulty of the test item considered in the ICC. It is of paramount importance that this theoretical notion of the separation of items from persons so germane to IRT be clearly understood for ICC methodology in test item bias work. All that follows rests squarely on this concept.

All ICCs are plotted from test data and form curves of the same general form: from left to right, beginning low, inclining sharply, and leveling off dramatically. Exceptions to this more or less S shape of the curve are uncommon. The S-shaped curves are called *ogives*. Ogives are merely a specialized graphic representation of a frequency distribution.

There are of course an infinite number of ogives, each dependent on the particular distribution described. If the values plot a perfectly smooth rising curve under very specified rules (e.g., ordinate axis is defined as a cumulative frequency), it is of the normal frequency function type and is called the *normal ogive*. Because of the anomalies of numbers, normal ogives are very difficult to work with mathematically. *Logistic ogives*, on the other hand, are much easier to handle mathematically and give a very close approximation to the normal ogives. Therefore, IRT deals with logistic ogives rather than with the normal frequency function.

There are a variety of mathematical approaches (and a logic behind each) to describe a particular ogive of an ICC. Some of the ways (called models) available to form the ICC are the *normal ogive model*, the *one-parameter logistic model*, the *two-parameter logistic model*, and the *three-parameter logistic model*. Another model, one of the most widely recognized, is the Rasch model; it is often referred to as the one-parameter logistic model and defined by others to be a special case of the two-parameter model (see Hambleton et al., 1978). There are still other models: the *nominal response model*, the *graded response model*, and the *continuous response model*. This list is certainly not exhaustive.

There is considerable psychometric debate about characteristics, advantages, and shortcomings of several of the models, but the three-parameter logistic model appears to receive the most favorable attention for bias item detection work. This may be because it comes closest to describing psychometrically multiple choice tests as they are presently constructed and used. Further exploration with IRT may develop fruitful results for test item bias work with various models, but for convenience this discussion will be limited to the three-parameter logistic model only.

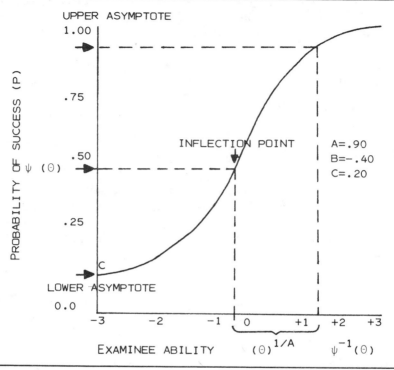

Figure 6: Hypothetical Three-Parameter Logistic Ogive with Characteristic Parts Labeled

The Three-Parameter Model

The three-parameter logistic model patterns the shape of the item characteristic curve for all the three possible item parameters: item discrimination, item difficulty, and psuedochance (i.e., guessing). In Figure 6, each of the characteristic parts for the three parameter logistic ogive is shown. The parameters are labeled a, b, and c for item discrimination, item difficulty, and pseudochance, respectively. (Figure 6 presents a logistic ogive, but in more detail, identical to the one in Figure 4.) Three things are to be especially noted in Figure 6, each of which requires some explanation. They are: (1) The slope of the curve is monotonic; that is, it always rises and is never exactly horizontal, (2) The inflection point; it is determined by the left to right and shift of the curve. (3) The two asymptotes, upper and lower, which may approach but never actually reach 1.00 and 0.00, respectively.

The a value, representing the first parameter, is the item discrimination. This value is related to the slope of the curve and it is fixed on a scale when an examinee has a 50% probability of correctly answering the item. It ranges from the interval $[-\infty, +\infty]$, although negative slopes are not relevant to our point. Typically, a values range from .5 to 2.5.

The b parameter is an index of difficulty and usually ranges from -2.5 to $+2.5$, with items of 0.0 b values about average difficulty. The b parameter describes the shift of the logistic ogive from left to right. An ogive predominately to the left of the θ scale denotes the item is generally easy for the examinees at the ability level. A shift to the right indicates a difficult item. A right-shifted ogive with a b value of $+2.5$ would indicate a very difficult item.

The c parameter, the pseudochance parameter, specifies the probability for an examinee of low ability of answering correctly a given item by simply guessing. This probability is described by the lower asymptote for the ICC. The probability of guessing an answer correctly is traditionally thought of in multiple choice tests as $1/A$, where A is the number of alternative answers to an item. In a four-choice test item, .25 is considered the probability of guessing correctly by chance ($1/4 = .25$). However, as we shall see, the lower asymptote of the ICC is seldom $1/A$. This is because in IRT it is presumed that examinees do not guess randomly when the correct answer choice is not positively know. Most c values range from .00 to .40. The lower the c value the better, indicating a low probability of getting the answer correct by merely the guessing of low ability examinees. Items with .30 or greater c values are considered not very good; c values of .20 or lower are desirable.

The technique for ICC item bias detection is to compare the differences in item characteristic curves for groups. The area between the equated ICCs is an indication of the degree of bias present in a considered test item. Several figures will add understanding by illustrating the point. Figure 7 presents ICCs for an item that exhibits bias between two groups in discrimination only (a). Figure 8 illustrates the shape of ICC curves for two groups indicating difficulty parameter bias (b). And Figure 9 displays for two groups the ICCs for an item exhibiting bias in both difficulty (b) and discrimination (a) parameters.

Estimation of the Parameters

The very practical problem of estimating values for each of the three parameters is mathematically complex, and computations will

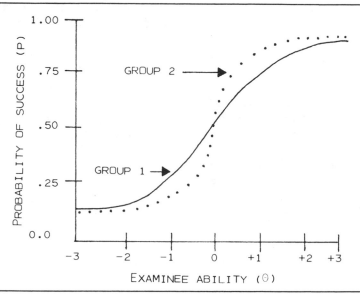

Figure 7: Hypothetical Equated Item Characteristic Curves for Two Groups Different in Discrimination

not be discussed here. The precise mathematics are detailed by Birnbaum (1968), and the advanced reader is referred to this excellent source. Nevertheless, understanding the process is extremely relevant to our use of ICC for items bias investigation.

It is often necessary to compute a large number of parameters, particularly if a long test with many items is administered to a large number of examinees. The number of parameters to be estimated is the ability parameters for each examinee and three times (once for each a, b, and c parameter) the number of items. If one follows Wood's (1976) recommendation, at least 1000 examinees and 30 to 40 items are needed in the test to get good estimates. In practice computer programs routinely perform the operation.

Two computer programs are available to estimate an examinee's θ according to the assumptions of the three parameter IRT model. One of these programs, named LOGIST, was written at the Educational Testing Service and is available from ETS (Wood et al., 1976). It uses a process of parameter estimation called maximum likelihood estimation procedures. The other program, called ANCILLES, uses a slightly different procedure called the Bayesian estimation method

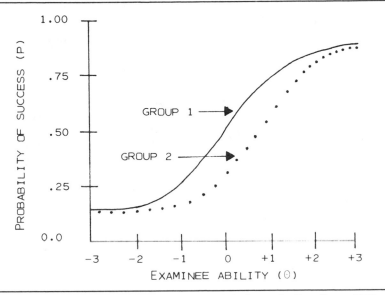

Figure 8: Hypothetical Equated Item Characteristic Curves for Two Groups Different in Difficulty

(ANCILLES is available from Dr. Vern Urry of the U.S. Civil Service Commission USCSC, 1978).

The LOGIST program is currently the most popular parameter estimation program in use, and it will be the only computer program discussed. LOGIST estimates all three parameters (a, b, c) simultaneously using the method of maximum likelihood estimation. This procedure is a series of repetitive (called iterative) computations. The iterative technique computes the first estimates for each parameter from raw scores. These first estimates become input for the second iteration. Then those estimates become input for the third iteration, and so on until the estimates converge. Again, the mathematics need not concern us directly; rather, it is the conceptual grasp of the process for estimation of parameters that is important.

By now it should be clear that the probability of a correct response at a given level increases monotonically as true ability increases. An examinee with a high true ability has a high probability of responding correctly to the considered item; and a low probability of correct response (i.e., approaching the lower asymptote of the curve) is given to an examinee of low true ability.

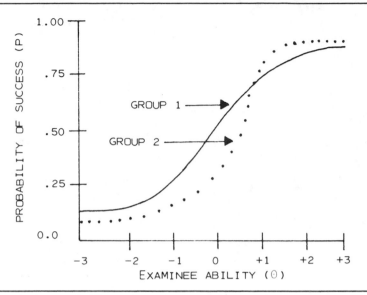

Figure 9: Hypothetical Equated Item Characteristic Curves for Two Groups Different in Discrimination, Difficulty, and Pseudochance

The following notation is used to indicate the probability of a correct response to item i given an examinee of ability level θ_j:

$$P(u_i = 1/\theta_j) \text{ or, more simply, } P(\theta_j)$$

The three parameter logistic model is represented as:

$$P(\theta_j) = c_i + (1 - c_i) [1 + \exp(-11.7a_i(\theta_j - b_i))] - 1 \qquad [20]$$

where: θ_j is on examinee's ability level

$P(\theta_j)$ is on the probability of a correct response at an examinee's ability level

a_i is the discrimination of item i

b_i is the difficulty of item i

c_i is an estimate of guessing for item i

Bias is estimated for an item by a difference in the ICCs for two groups when θ is equated. Let us refer again to Figures 7, 8, and 9. In the figures ICCs have been computed for each of two groups. When θ values are equated (that is, both groups are placed on the same scale) it can be seen that different probabilities result for each group. Bias is then inferred for the item. For example, consider Figure 7. An examinee of θ value zero has a 50% probability of a correct response on the item in either group. This item cannot be considered unbiased, however, because at any other θ value the probabilities for a correct response are different for each group. The probability for a correct response for Group 1 is greater than that for Group 2 when comparatively low θ values are considered, but the opposite occurs for examinees of high θ values. The item does not discriminate equally between the two groups, and it is inferred that bias is present. Bias is also exhibited in the ICCs of Figure 8. 50% probability of a correct response is not present when θs are equated. This item discriminates in difficulty. The example may likewise be discontinued for the ICCs in Figure 9, where the effects of bias are confounded for both discrimination and difficulty.

Equating the Scales

After parameter estimates have been obtained for each of two groups, two steps remain for the completion of the bias item detection procedure: equating the scales and comparing the curves. Each step will be dealt with separately; there are a number of procedures available for both. When parameters for items are estimated, whether by the maximum likelihood procedure or another method, they will not be identical when different samples are used for parameterization. Although both groups are on essentially the same scale, they differ by a linear transformation. This occurs because in each instance of parameterization θ is defined with 0 as a mean and 1 as the standard deviation. In other words, the parameters a_i and b_i are invariant from group to group, but they are not invariant when the origin for θ is arbitrarily changed for each parameterization. Such is the case regardless of the examinees' true ability when compared to an outside criterion or any amount of dispersion of ability within groups. The scales' difference must therefore be equated when parameters are estimated for each of two dichotomous groups. When the θ scales are equated, meaningful comparisons of the ICCs between different groups are possible.

The scale for one group may be equated to another by the simple linear transformation $Y = ax + b$. The second group's item parameters may be equated with two formulas. These formulas are:

$$a_{i2}^* = (1/A)\, a_{i2} \qquad [21]$$

and:

$$b_{i2}^* = A\, b_{i2} + B \qquad [22]$$

where * denotes an equated parameter, i is the considered item, and the second subscript represents which group was used to obtain the parameter estimates. The A and B values are constants such that the mean and variance of the transformed b's of the second group are equal to the mean and variance of the first group. If the assumption of unidimensionality is perfectly satisfied, then:

$$A = \sigma_{b_{i1}} / \sigma_{b_{i2}} \qquad [23]$$

where $\sigma_{b_{i2}}$ is the standard deviation of the difficulty parameter (b_i) for Group 1, and b_{i2} is the equivalent for Group 2. Realistically, perfection in unidimensionality is rarely achieved. The logistic ogive is usually compressed or elongated depending on whether A is greater than one ($A > 1$) or less than one ($A < 1$), respectively.

Also, the ogive shift from left to right is dictated by the value for constant B being greater than or less than zero ($B > 0$), respectively. This constant may be determined from:

$$B = b_{.1} - Ab_{.2} \qquad [24]$$

where $b_{.1}$ represents the mean item difficulty for Group 1 and $b_{.2}$ denotes the equivalent value for Group 2. The θ values follow the simple linear transformation given earlier.

Different schools of thought exist for the transformation of c parameter estimates since it is commonly held that neither of the two popularly used computer programs for parameter estimation (i.e., LOGIST and ANCILLES) properly estimates the pseudochance probabilities. One notion suggests that no transformation of the estimates for c_i is required at all. An alternative technique is offered in which one replaces the c_i parameter estimates for one group with those obtained for the second group. This fixes the c_i value for each group with the lower of the two groups' pseudoguessing parameter estimates placed at the bottom.

Comparing the Curves

Comparing the ICCs for two groups different by some independent variable (e.g., ethnic heritage, sex) is the final step in using the three-parameter logistic model of IRT for item analysis in test item bias work. When the equated ICCs are identical for both groups, it is taken as an indication of freedom within the item from systematic error in the estimation of item discrimination, item difficulty, and pseudochance-level guessing for low ability examinees. Bias is inferred any time equated ICCs are not identical. As one can easily imagine, there a number of techniques for comparing the curves. Since this discussion is limited to three-parameter logistic model solely, only comparisons appropriate to this model will be discussed. And, again, only ICCs that have been equated may be meaningfully compared.

Simply eyeballing differences in space between the ICCs for two groups can be an effective strategy for comparing the two curves (Rudner, 1977). Comparing the ICCs for a number of items in this way (each on a separate chart) will give a visual picture of the differences and an indication of which items show a relatively greater degree of disparity among groups.

Inferential procedures are also available for comparing curves. When using these procedures, bias may be said to exist in some degree when a difference between the ICCs is noted among any of four areas. They are: (1) the absolute difference between ICCs, (2) the area, if any, where the ICC for Group 1 is above that of Group 2, (3) the obverse—the area, if any, where the ICC for Group 2 is above that of Group 1, and (4) the square root of the sum of the squared differences between ICCs (Linn et al., 1981). Arbitrary limits for each case may be drawn to bound the areas. These criteria are arbitrary because no specific significance test is available to test differences between estimates of area.

The formula to compare the area between two equated ICCs may be represented mathematically as:

$$\phi_i = \sum_{-5.000}^{5.000} [/P(u_i = 1/\theta_j) - P'(u_i = 1/\theta_j)] \, \Delta\theta \qquad [25]$$

where $\Delta\theta = .005$, and $P(u_i = 1/\theta_j)$ and $P'(u_j = 1/\theta_j)$ are the equated parameters for two groups.

If all of the assumptions of IRT are perfectly met—that is, the test is unidimensional, local independence for items exists, and the test also has error-free estimates for the three parameters of the item characteristic curve—the equated ICCs would be equal, and the area between them would be zero (i.e., $\theta_j = 0$). $\theta_j > 0$ is an indication of bias. Usually this indicates that the unidimensionality assumption is not equally valid for both groups of examinees and that the items measure different traits across the independent variable selected for dichotomization, or possibly the inappropriateness of the item for the trait measure.

A troublesome problem may, on occasion, occur when comparing the area between ICCs for equated groups many times. It is possible for there to be no practical difference in the ICCs yet item parameters may be substantially different. This observation can occur, for example, when there is an extraordinarily high b parameter estimate for one group. Procedures for placing confidence bands around the ICCs may overcome this anomaly.

What Researchers Think of ICC

Several important studies of test item bias have used the three-parameter ICC methodology. Since IRT has only recently been applied as a biased item detection strategy, these studies are quite fresh. In one study, Rudner (1980a) investigated the three-parameter ICC strategy as a methodology per se rather than as an investigation into bias in a particular test. Using the ICC with items from a Monte Carlo-generated item pool, Rudner concluded that the three-parameter ICC approach produced satisfactory results (compared with other medhodologies) under each of the test conditions.

In an earlier and very interesting study (Rudner, 1978) using the three-parameter ICC approach, item bias was investigated for equivalent measures with two different populations: reading achievement for a hearing-imparied population of students versus reading achievement for normal hearing students. Again, the ICC approach was judged to be an attractive and appropriate bias detection methodology. And there are numerous studies of test item bias using ICC methods with racial or ethnic heritage as the independent variable (Ironson and Subkoviak, 1979; Linn et al., 1981; Lord, 1977b; Osterlind and Martois, 1981). The consensus of conclusions from these studies is that the ICC approach is the most generally valid of all biased item detection methods. Thus it can be seen that despite its computational complexities, ICC methodology is a valuable tool in item bias detection work.

6. DISTRACTOR RESPONSE ANALYSIS

Distractor response analysis (distractor) is the final test item bias procedure to be discussed. Examining the incorrect alternatives to a test item—usually termed *distractors* but sometimes called *question foils*—for differences in patterns of response among different subgroups of a population is the essential strategy of the distractor response analysis technique. The function of distractor is to determine the significance of the differences among two or more groups' response frequencies in the discrete categories of question distractors. If a significance test reveals that two or more groups distinguished by some criterion are in fact differentially attracted to a test item's distractors, the null hypothesis (of no difference in the groups' relative frequencies for distractors) may be rejected, and bias is inferred to be present.

The attraction of the distractor approach to the detection of test item bias lies at the surface. If one group differs in percentage of correct response (p value) on an item from another group, and by a wide margin, it is a natural curiosity point to explore the distractors for patterns of response. Obvious patterns of responses are usually found. The percentage of responses to each question distractor is very seldom the same or even nearly the same; typically, one or another specific distractor will account for a large percentage of the incorrect responses to a test item. Also, on retest, examinees respond to the same incorrect choice with remarkable stability. this is presumed to be so because in a test appropriate for a particular ability group rarely is an examinee completely bamboozled with no notion at all about any of the distractors. Distractors are carefully constructed by test developers to present attractive features for test takers, and studies have verified that when an examinee incorrectly responds to a test question, the reaction is seldom pure guessing or random choice (see Lord, 1980; Warm, 1978). Incorrect choices are usually a "best guess" about which there is at least some known information or some incorrectly held information. The examination of the incorrect response alternative, concomitant with an appropriate statistical test for data analysis, is the concept of distractor.

The distractor approach focuses attention only on response alternatives; there is no assessment of the item stem (i.e., wording of the question statement) or directions for answering. Nor does distractor response analysis investigate test-taking strategies or techniques, such as preparedness, using an answer sheet rather than responding directly on the test booklet, extraneous noise or other disturbing conditions, and the like. Also omitted from analysis are blanks and questions for which no examinee response at all was given. Typically, such blanks become increasingly frequent toward the end of a test. This may indicate that examinees did not have sufficient time to complete the test. "Speededness" of tests is a variable not investigated by distractor. However, the same cannot be said for double marks, questions for which an examinee answered with two alternatives. Such responses are counted as incorrect, regardless of the choices selected. The rationale given by most test developers are counting double marks as incorrect is that examinees are presumably "playing the odds" rather than displaying full question knowledge.

Distractor response analysis is generally not recommended for use with tests having only two response alternatives or for true/false questions since the reliability of the test score is comparatively low. Some scoring techniques that account for right, wrong, and unanswered items, as well as minimize the effects of guessing, can improve reliability; however, use of distractor is still discouraged with such two-choice questions because of the very limited amount of information yielded.

The Procedures

The first step in the distractor procedure to investigate biased items is to prepare a matrix of choice-response alternatives for the test items under consideration. Such an arrangement of data is displayed in Table 4. In the study three groups were identified, and the item had four response alternatives: the correct choice, C, and three distractors, A, B, and D. Note that Table 4 presents not only distractors to the question, but also the correct answer choice. The number of examinees with double marks is noted too. The next step is to place the data in a series of 2xk contingency tables to prepare for significance testing. Table 5 presents these tables for the data described in Table 4.

Veale and Foreman (1975) originally proposed a strategy for investigating question distractors based on chi-square procedures in which only the incorrect choices are considered. This procedure is not

TABLE 4
Choice-Response Matrix for One Test Item

Groups	A	B	C*	D	Double Marks	Omits	Total
1	32	32	56	16	12	0	136
2	24	72	40	24	16	0	176
3	24	5	8	6	4	0	47

*Correct answer.

recommended because when one ignores the correct choice alternative, the resultant statistic will not distribute as a true χ^2, and spurious conclusions could follow. Therefore, a series of 2xk contingency tables must be established to account for all the available data on any particular item.

A cursory examination of Table 5 reveals an obvious pull for Group 3 examinees on distractor A, and Group 2 examinees on distractor B. But visual analysis is not sufficient to conclude bias for the item; there must also be empirical verification. This means hypotheses testing.

The hypothesis under test by the distractor approach is one of comparing conditional probabilities between groups on question response alternatives. The probabilities may be expressed as:

$$P_{ibk}$$

where i is the particular group considered, b is the response alternative, and k is the response level (correct or incorrect). And generally stated:

$$i = 1, 2, \ldots, I$$

$$b = 1, 2, \ldots, B$$

and:

$$k = 1, \text{ if the response is correct}$$

$$k = 2, \text{ if the response in correct}$$

TABLE 5
Contingency Tables for Three Groups on Distractors to One Test Item

DISTRACTOR A

GROUPS	1	2	3
+	49.74 / 56	36.17 / 40	18.09 / 8
0	38.26 / 32	27.83 / 24	13.91 / 24

$$\chi^2_A = 15.68 \ (p < .01)$$

DISTRACTOR B

GROUPS	1	2	3
+	42.97 / 56	54.69 / 40	6.35 / 8
0	45.03 / 32	57.31 / 72	6.65 / 5

$$\chi^2_B = 16.27 \ (p < .01)$$

DISTRACTOR D

GROUPS	1	2	3
+	49.92 / 56	44.37 / 40	9.71 / 8
0	22.08 / 16	19.63 / 24	4.29 / 6

$$\chi^2_D = 4.80$$

DOUBLE MARKS

GROUPS	1	2	3
+	52.00 / 56	42.82 / 40	9.18 / 8
0	16.00 / 12	13.18 / 16	2.82 / 4

$$\chi^2_{DM} = 2.74$$

+ = success on item.
0 = failure on item.

Thus the pairwise comparisons for three separate groups may be considered by the hypotheses:

$H_{0(1)}: P_{1b2} = P_{2b2}$ $H_{1(1)}: P_{1b2} \neq P_{2b2}$

$H_{0(2)}: P_{1b2} = P_{3b2}$ $H_{2(2)}: P_{1b2} \neq P_{3b2}$

$H_{0(3)}: P_{2b2} = P_{3b2}$ $H_{3(3)}: P_{2b2} \neq P_{3b2}$

The pairwise statements are simply the comparison between groups for each question alternative. For a particular distractor to be considered unbiased, the probabilities for any group to select that distractor must be equal.

Significance Tests

There are several statistical tests available to distractor procedures given the generalized hypothesis under consideration. In large sample situations a two-way contingency table is investigated by the usual chi statistic for two independent samples. Degrees of freedom may be calculated in the normal manner (i.e., $\gamma = [r - 1][k - 1]$). Bias is inferred for unequal distribution of distractor responses when the χ^2 value exceeds a predetermined level of significance. When the sample size is small (e.g., cell sizes are less than five), the Fisher exact probability test is recommended.

The total significance level may be partitioned across the number of tests to be performed. this helps to control for Type 1 errors. (The same reasoning we used earlier with Marascuilo Method One of the chi-square strategy for investigating bias in items at several ability levels.) Symbolically stated, this is:

$$\alpha = \frac{1}{b} \, \alpha_t \qquad\qquad [26]$$

If there are three incorrect response alternatives (and a fourth possibility for double marks), the case for the item displayed in Table 5, and the significance level for the total item is set at .05, then

$$\alpha = \tfrac{1}{4}(.05) = .0125$$

Taking the data in Table 5, the critical χ^2 value for any particular distractor at .0125 with 2 degrees of freedom (i.e., $\gamma = 2$) is 9.21. Therefore, bias for the item may be inferred by a χ^2 value exceeding the 9.21 tabled critical value at any response alternative. In this example bias is inferred for the item by $\chi_A^2 = 15.68$ and $\chi_B^2 = 16.27$.

One final note needs mention. Although these data are adapted from a real bias study, they represent only a hypothetical case. In order to apply the goodness-of-fit test to a set of "live" data, combining some classes may be necessary to make sure each expected frequency is not too small (say, not less than five). Or, when only two groups are compared and $\gamma = 1$, and when any expected frequency is less than 10, Yates's correction for continuity should be applied.

Post Hoc Procedures

With large samples and a chi-square test for goodness of fit of observed data to expected frequencies a follow-up procedure is recommended. The check is to ensure the heterogeneity of response distribution across groups. Cramer's V statistic is the appropriate test (Veale and Foreman, 1975). It is:

$$V = \sqrt{\frac{\chi^2}{N \min(r - 1, k - 1)}} \qquad [27]$$

This is, the square root of the chi-square value divided by the product of the number of examinees in the population and the minimum degrees of freedom allowed.

Or, for an entire test instrument, a generalized form of Cramer's V may be given as follows:

$$V_t = \sqrt{\frac{\sum\limits_{i=1}^{I} \chi^2}{\sum\limits_{i=1}^{I} N_i \min(r_i - 1, k_i - 1)}} \qquad [28]$$

Both V and V assume the range [0, +1]. Lower V or V values correspond to a greater degree of homogeneity, that is, lesser association between groups and distractors. This is useful information in bias studies when distractor response is of particular interest.

The Cramer's V statistic as well as the usual chi-square function adequately when the size of the samples considered is large. But when the samples are small (e.g., $N < 40$), the cells of the contingency table for observed distractor responses may be quite small. If the number of cells in the contingency table with an expected frequency of less than five observations exceeds 20% of the total number of cells, the chi-square approximation of the sampling distribution is not sufficiently close, and neither the chi square nor either form of Cramer's V is recommended.

When it is possible by rationale of an external criterion, groups may be combined to increase cell size to the recommended minimum. This combining of scores is usually done by averaging the values for the groups' distractors over the items comprising the instrument and using the number of examinees missing the items as weights.

If by pooling categories it is still not possible to approximate the sampling distribution with the χ^2 statistic, the Kolmogorov-Smirnov test may be preferred. This test is concerned with the degree of agreement between two sets of values. The essential consideration of the Kolmogorov-Smirnov two-sample test is whether two independent samples have been drawn from the same population. When two groups of examinees are in fact representative of the same population (or from populations with the same distribution), the cumulative distributions of both groups may be expected to be fairly close to each other on the assumption that each should exhibit only random deviation from the overall population distribution.

The Kolmogorov Smirnov test is a two-tailed test in bias item detection strategies and may be represented as follows:

$$D = \max [S_{n1}(X) - S_{n2}(X)] \qquad [29]$$

where:

$S_{n1}(X)$ = the observed cumulative step function of one group (i.e., $S_{n1}(X) = K/_{ni}$ where K = the number of scores equal to or less than (X)

and:

$S_{n2}(X)$ = analogous values to $S_{n1}(S)$ for the second group

By equation 29 the absolute value of D is found irrespective of direction. For small samples the significance levels for rejection of the hypothesis under consideration must be read from a table of critical values where the sampling distribution of D is known.

A procedure for investigating bias within the total test instrument is also available. Conceptually, it is the sum of findings for the individual item hypotheses testings. To test the combined hypotheses for all items in a test, simply sum the individual chi squares for each item considered. This may be represented as follows:

$$\chi^2_t = \sum_{i=1}^{I} \chi^2_i \qquad [30]$$

where I is the number of items in the test. This χ^2 will distribute as a normal χ^2 by the rule of additivity and will have $\Sigma_i (r_i - 1)(k_i - 1)$ degrees of freedom. In this case if the χ^2 value exceeds the tabled value for significance at the desired confidence level, the entire test may be said to exhibit bias.

Because of its comparative ease of technique, as well as its conceptual simplicity, the distractor approach to detecting test item bias is useful in many settings. For example, distractor techniques may be helpful to test constructors. The initial screening of response choice alternatives for potential bias can contribute much to construct validity for items. Distractor may also be used in research settings. One suggestion here may be to examine total test items by another of the biased item detection strategies first, and then further interrogate items identified as biased with the distractor approach. Other contexts in which the strategy may be successfully exploited will become evident with its increased use.

7. SUMMARY

This monograph has presented five strategies for exploring the psychometric properties of test items for systematic errors in measurement, or bias. Throughout the discussions a common criterion for bias was maintained: i.e., a test item is said to be unbiased when the probability for success on the item is the same for equally able examinees of the same population regardless of their subgroup membership. Despite their common purpose and adherence to a uniform criterion for bias, the five strategies are not alike in scope or approach. Each technique offers a slightly different conceptual perspective, and there are considerable differences among the procedures in computation and interpretation. The decision of which procedure to use and when should be guided by the answers to a number of questions: What are the hypotheses under test? Are the sample size adequate for the statistics employed? Are computers and appropriate programs required and available? How might the results be interpreted to a given audience? These questions, and others, should be addressed before beginning an investigation into item bias.

The ANOVA approach examines only the interaction of groups $\times$ items and presumes this is a valid indicator of bias within items. The TID strategy also accepts this assumption and takes the procedures a step further by identifying individual items with pronounced values in the interaction. The focus of attention for both approaches is solely on item difficulty. This fact presents several problems, not the least of which is that groups $\times$ item interaction can occur in any test regardless of item bias. The chi-square approaches attempt to avoid this troublesome spur by examining differences in proportions across total score categories. The χ^2 approach is comparatively simple to compute, but had the disadvantage of the arbitrary selection of ability levels.

Item characteristic curve approaches are certainly the most elegant and technically sophisticated of all the strategies discussed. They can give an indication of item difficulty, item discrimination, and some guessing levels. However, their very elegance can also be a hindrance because they require a high degree of technical know-how for both the computation and interpretation. Also, a very large sample is required for the ICC approach.

Lastly, the distractor approach, like chi square, also examines a difference in proportions. However, with distractor the attention is focused on the incorrect answer choices to a test item. This procedure seeks to reveal whether or not there is a differential pull toward question distractors between groups.

These comments are summarized in Table 6. This table is meant to be a quick reference to the procedures; certainly much is omitted for economy of space, and the reader is cautioned against using it without having first read the complete description for the procedures.

Naturally, the reader may be curious to know the consistency across administrations of various item bias investigation techniques. There

TABLE 6
Summary of Selected Item Bias Detection Techniques

Method	Focus of Analysis	Aspect Examined	Computation Ease	Computational Aids Necessary	Ease of Interpretation	Measure of Bias	Sample Size Needed
ANOVA	Interaction between group membership and correct response	Item Difficulty	Difficult	Computer Necessary	Moderate to Difficult	Significance of F main effects and interactions	Depends on the number of items; conservative, 100 per group
TID	Interaction between group membership and correct response	Item Difficulty	Simple	Hand Calculation, Possible Calculator Desirable, Computer Handy	Simple	Arbitrary designation of distance on scatterplot	30 to 50 people per group

CHI	Difference in proportions attaining a correct response across total score categories	Item Difficulty	Moderate to Simple	Hand Calculation, Possible Calculator Desirable, Computer Handy	Simple	Significance of chi square	100 or more per group
ICC	Difference in probability of responding correctly	Item Difficulty, Item Discrimination, Guessing	Difficult	Computer Necessary	Difficult	Area between ICC curves	Conservative, 1000 per group
DISTRACTOR	Difference in proportions selecting distractors	Distractor Difficulty	Simple	Hand Calculation, Possible Calculator Desirable, Computer Handy	Simple	Significance of chi square	100 or more per group

SOURCE: W. R. Merz (1980) Methods of Assessing Bias and Fairness in Tests. ARC Technical Report IZI-79. Sacramento, CA. Reprinted by permission.

have been a number of comparative studies of item bias methods (see Burrill, 1982; Ironson and Subkoviak, 1979; Merz and Grossen, 1979; Rudner et al., 1980a). The general thrust of these comparisons has been to determine the adequacy of the procedures. Each of the procedures described in this monograph will satisfactorily serve its intended purpose. Since each approach is conceptually unique and is available to interrogate specific and different hypotheses, it is not appropriate to judge the adequacy of them by looking for identical test items to be identified by various techniques.

As was emphasized in Chapter 1, bias within test items is not an objectively defined noun that can be seen and caught and eliminated. Rather, bias in psychological tests is merely the presence, to one degree or another, of a specific kind of error in measurement: the over- or underestimation of a population parameter. The techniques described in this monograph, when properly used, will aid in reducing errors in measurement. To this limited extent an understanding of test item bias and knowledge of appropriate strategies to detect such systematic errors in measurement will serve the common good of well-constructed tests.

REFERENCES

American Psychological Association (1974) Standards for Educational and Psychological Tests.

ANGOFF, W. H. (1972) "A technique for the investigation of cultural differences." Presented at the Annual Meeting of the American Psychological Association, May, Honolulu. (ERIC Document Reproduction Service ED 069 686.)

——— and S. F. FORD (1973) "Item-race interaction on a test of scholastic aptitude." Journal of Educational Measurement 10: 95-105.

BAKER, F. B. (1981) "A criticism of Scheuneman's item bias technique." Journal of Educational Measurement 18: 59-62.

——— (1977) "Advances in item analysis." Review of Educational Research 47: 151-178.

BINET, A. and T. SIMON (1916) The Development of Intelligence in Children. (Elizabeth S. Kite, trans.). Baltimore: Williams & Wilkins.

BIRNBAUM, A. (1968) "Some latent trait models and their use in inferring an examinee's ability," in F. M. Lord and M. R. Novik (eds.) Statistical Theories of Mental Test Scores. Reading, MA: Addison-Wesley.

BURRILL, L. E. (1982) "Comparative studies of item bias methods," pp. 161-179 in R. A. Berk (ed.) Handbook of Methods for Detecting Test Bias. Baltimore, MD: Johns Hopkins University Press.

CARDALL, C. and W. E. COFFMAN (1964) A Method for Comparing the Performance of Different Groups on the Items in a Test. College Entrance Examination Board Research and Development Report 64-5, No. 9. Research Bulletin 64-61 (November). Princeton, NJ: Educational Testing Service.

CLEARY, T. A. and T. L. HILTON (1968) "An investigation of item bias." Educational and Psychological Measurement 28: 61-75.

CRONBACH, L. J. (1976) "Equity in selection—where psychometrics and political philosophy meet." Journal of Educational Measurement 13: 31-42.

DIAMOND, E. E. (1981) "Item bias issues: background, problems and where we are today." Presented at the Annual Meeting of the American Educational Research Association, April, Los Angeles.

ECHTERNACHT, G. A. (1974) "A quick method for determining test bias." Educational and Psychological Measurement 34: 271-280.

EELLS, K., A. DAVIS, R. J. HAVIGHURST, V. E. HERRICK, and R. W. TYLER (1951) Intelligence and Cultural Differences. Chicago: University of Chicago Press.

FLAUGHER, R. L. (1978) "The many definitions of test bias." American Psychologist 3: 671-679.

GREEN, D. R. and J. F. DRAPER (1972) "Exploratory studies of bias in achievement tests." Presented at the Annual Meeting of the American Psychological Association, September, Honolulu. (ERIC Document Reproduction Service ED 070 794).

HAMBLETON, R. K. (1979) "Latent trait models and their applications," pp. 13-32 in R. Traub (ed.) New Directions for Testing and Measurement, Vol. 4: Methodological Developments. San Francisco: Jossey-Bass.

————and H. SWAMINATHAN, L. L. COOK, D. R. EIGNOR, and J. A. GIFFORD (1978) "Developments in latent trait theory: models, technical issues, and applications." Review of Educational Research 48: 467-510.

HUNTER, J. E. (1975) "A critical analysis of the use of item means and item-test correlations to determine the presence or absence of content bias in achievement test items." Presented at the National Institute of Education Conference on Test Bias, December, Annapolis, Maryland.

IRONSON, G. H. and M. J. SUBKOVIAK (1979) "A comparison of several methods of assessing item bias." Journal of Educational Measurement 16: 209-225.

JENSEN, A. R. (1980) Bias in Mental Testing. New York: Free Press.

LINN, R. L. (1981) "Item bias in a test of reading comprehension." Applied Psychological Measurement 5 (Spring): 159-173.

————and M. V. LEVINE, C. N. HASTINGS, and J. L. WARDROP (1981) An Investigation of Item Bias in a Test of Reading Comprehension. ERIC Document Reproduction Service ED 184 091.

LORD, F. M. (1980) Applications of Item Response Theory to Practical Testing Problems. Hillsdale, NJ: Erlbaum.

————(1977a) "Practical applications of item characteristic curve theory." Journal of Educational Measurement 14: 117-138.

————(1977b) "A study of item bias using item characteristic curve theory," pp. 19-29 in N. H. Poortinga (ed.) Basic Problems in Cross-Cultural Psychology. Amsterdam: Swits & Vitlinger.

————(1952) "A theory of test scores." Psychometric Monograph No. 7 Psychometric Society.

————and M. R. NOVICK (1974) Statistical Theories of Mental Test Scores. Reading, MA: Addison-Wesley.

MARASCUILO, L. A. (1971) Statistical Methods for Behavioral Science Research. New York: McGraw-Hill.

————and R. E. SLAUGHTER (1981a) "Statistical procedures for analyzing item bias based on chi square statistics." Presented at the Annual Meeting of the American Educational Research Association, April, Los Angeles.

————(1981b) "Statistical procedures for identifying possible sources of item bias based on X^2 statistics." Journal of Educational Measurement 18: 229-248.

MARASCUILO, L. A. and M. MCSWEENEY (1977) Nonparametric and Distribution Free Methods for the Social Sciences. Monterey, CA: Brooks/Cole.

MERZ, W. R. (1978) "Test fairness and test bias: a review of procedures," pp. 129-151 in M. Wargo and D. R. Green (eds) Achievement Testing of Disadvantaged and Minority Students for Educational Program Evaluation. Monterey, CA: McGraw-Hill.

————and N. GROSSEN (1979) "An empirical investigation of six methods for examining test item bias." Presented at the Annual Meeting of the National Council on Measurement in Education, April. (ERIC Document Reproduction Service ED 178 566).

NUNNALLY, J. C. (1978) Psychometric Theory. New York: McGraw-Hill.

National Research Council, Committee on Ability Testing, Assembly of Behavioral Social Sciences (1982) Ability testing: Uses, Consequences, and Controversies, Parts I and II. Washington, DC: National Academy Press.

On Bias in Selection (1976) Special issue, Journal of Educational Measurement 13: 1-100.

OSTERLIND, S. J. and J. MARTOIS (1981) Latent Trait Theory Applications to Test Item Bias Methodology. Research Memorandum, Oakland Unified School District, Oakland, CA. (ERIC Document Reproduction Service ED 206 650).

PETERSON, N. S. and M. R. NOVICK (1976) "An evaluation of some models for culture fair selection." Journal of Educational Measurement 13: 3-29.

PINE, S. M. (1977) "Applications of item response theory to the problem of test bias," in D. J. Weiss (ed.) Applications of Computerized Adaptive Testing. Research Report 77-1. Minneapolis: University of Minnesota, Psychometric Methods Program, Department of Psychology.

PLAKE, B. S. (1981) "An ANOVA methodology to identify biased test items that takes instructional level into account." Educational and Psychological Measurement 41: 365-368.

RUDNER, L. M. (1978) "Using standard tests with the hearing impaired: the problem of item bias." Volta Review 80: 31-40.

——— (1977) "An evaluation of select approaches for biased item identification." Ph.D. dissertation, Catholic University of America, Washington, D.C.

——— P. R. GETSON, and D. L. KNIGHT (1980a) "A Monte Carlo comparison of seven biased item detection techniques." Journal of Educational Measurement 17: 1-10.

——— (1980b) "Biased item detection techniques." Journal of Educational Statistics 5: 213-233.

SCHEUNEMAN, J. D. (1979) "A method of assessing bias in test items." Journal of Educational Measurement 16: 143-152.

SHEPARD, L., G. CAMILLI, and M. AVERILL (1980) "Comparison of six procedures for detecting test item bias using both internal and external ability criteria." Presented at the meeting of the National Council on Measurement in Education, April, Boston.

STRICKER, L. J. (1981) A New Index of Differential Subgroup Performance: Application to the GRE Aptitude Test. GRE Research Report 78-7. Princeton, NJ: Educational Testing Service.

——— (1982) "Identifying test items that perform differentially in population subgroups: A partial correlation index." Applied Psychological Measurement 6: 261-273.

THURSTONE, L. L. (1925) "A method of scaling educational and psychological tests." Journal of Educational Psychology 16: 263-278.

URRY, V. (1978) ANCILLES: Item Parameter Estimation Program with Ogive and Logistic Three-Parameter Options." Washington, DC: U.S. Civil Service Commission, Personnel Research and Development Center.

VEALE, J. R. and D. I. FOREMAN (1975) Cultural Validity of Items and Tests: A New Approach. Score Technical Report. Iowa City, IA: Westinghouse Learning Corporation/Measurement Research Center.

WARM, T. A. (1978) A Primer of Item Response Theory. Technical Report 941078. Oklahoma City: U.S. Coast Guard Institute, Department of Transportation (NTIS AD A063072).

WINER, B. J. (1962) Statistical Principles in Experimental Design. New York: McGraw-Hill.

WOOD, R. L. and F. M. LORD (1976) A User's Guide to LOGIST. Research Memorandum. Princeton, NJ: Educational Testing Service.

——— M. S. WINGERSKY, and F. M. LORD (1976) LOGIST: A Computer Program for Estimating Examinee Ability and Item Characteristic Curve Parameters. Research Memorandum. Princeton, NJ: Educational Testing Service.

STEVEN J. OSTERLIND is Director of Research and Evaluation for the Oakland, California, Unified School District. He is coauthor of Evaluation Resource Handbook *and has published widely in the field of tests and measurement. In addition to his administrative duties, he is active in professional organizations: Board Member of Evaluation Network, Board Member of California Educational Research Association, and past president of California Association of Program Evaluators. He received his Ph.D. from the University of Southern California in 1976 and is a former American Scholar's Fellow at Yale University.*

Quantitative Applications in the Social Sciences

A SAGE UNIVERSITY PAPER SERIES

$13.95 each

To order, please use order form on the next page.

Quantitative Applications in the Social Sciences

A SAGE UNIVERSITY PAPER SERIES

$13.95 each

SAGE PUBLICATIONS, INC.
P.O. BOX 5084
THOUSAND OAKS, CALIFORNIA 91359-9924

Place
Stamp
here